Trust Your Heart

Spirit-Led Business

Practical Guide from a Christian Mom of Six and Her 30 Years of In-Home Business

by Marnie Pehrson Kuhns

Spirit-Led Business is the fourth book in the
Trust Your Heart Series.
Find other titles in the series at
www.TrustYourHeartSeries.com

Cover Image Copyright: Mo_Ali /
BigStockPhoto.com

Published by Spirit Tree Publishing
Imprint: Independently Published

514 Old Hickory Ln * Ringgold GA 30736
www.SpiritTreePublishing.com

ISBN: 9781659243505

Library of Congress Control Number: 2020900549

*Dedicated to those who care enough
to light the way for others.*

Table of Contents

Acknowledgements

I would like to give a special thanks to my friends and colleagues who have taught me so much over the years. I am incredibly grateful for those I mention by name in the book and those I have not named specifically. This book would not be possible without each person who has touched my life. I'd also like to acknowledge and thank my husband, David Kuhns, for his content editing and feedback on the flow of the book. Also, thank you to Joyce Pierce for proofreading the final manuscript. If there are errors, I'm sure they are ones I introduced as I formatted the final version.

Introduction

Since May 1990, I've had my own business doing computer training, marketing consulting, web design, programming, book authoring, book coaching, content marketing, public relations, advertising consulting, and more. I've even dabbled in a couple of multi-level marketing companies. Currently, I use music and energy therapy to help people tap into what their heart knows and the gifts they have. As a coach, I help them express themselves fully in the world and make the impact they're here to make.

You might be wondering how I went from such a technical business to something emotional, or "spiritual." In short, the Spirit led me there. Over the years, I've learned many lessons – the most important of which is to lean on the Spirit and follow its lead.

This book is for you if you often feel inspired nudges or outright inspiration about what to do or say, or how to be. It's for you if you have (or want to have) a business that makes a difference in the world while being true to who you are and having fun and fulfillment in the process. It's for you if you have lots of ideas and sometimes get distracted or have difficulty choosing a niche or one idea to pursue.

It's for you if you're tired of having to try so hard, having to stress about reaching your goals, or struggling in your business.

I'm writing this book because I know how you feel! In the pages that follow, I'll share my own story of how I got started in business and how the vast array of experiences I've had have served me. How I went from a stressed-out, workaholic mother of 6 running a home-based business, to a life where I spend most of my day doing what brings me joy.

I've learned this truth: Nothing is ever wasted if we can learn from it. Every path I've taken has taught me something valuable. In this book I'll share some of the important lessons I've learned over the last 30 years in business. I hope you'll find them helpful and that they provide insight and encouragement to lead your own Spirit-led business.

Within the pages of this book, you will discover how to:

- Tap into inspiration in a powerful way
- Get answers to your pressing problems
- Value yourself and not sell yourself short
- Get a clear direction, stay focused and stick with it
- Prosper with multiple income streams
- Leverage the power of relationships and collaboration to magnify your influence and success
- Act when inspiration comes
- Work in harmony with your natural rhythm (aka creative cycle) and understand where you are at any given point within it
- Be true to yourself and who you are

When the Spirit Sets You on A Path

In my early twenties, I started out as a stay-at-home mom who had majored in information management in college. I'd been taught cutting-edge database design techniques and implemented them on-the-job as I worked my way through college. After college, my husband lost his job. He suggested that, with my skills, I should try to find employment.

At the time, we had two children under two years old. I still remember the day I came home from an interview for a job and had the words enter my mind, "If you go to work outside the home, you'll never come home again." The Spirit knew what my conscious mind did not – that the dynamic in my marriage would result in my carrying the financial burden for the family if I went to work fulltime.

That spiritual message gave me the courage to implement an idea that had been simmering in my mind for some time. I had an idea that I could offer computer lessons from my home the way some people offer piano lessons. I called the local newspaper and placed an ad in the help wanted section that went something like this:

> "Are you being turned down for jobs
> because you don't know
> WordPerfect, Lotus or PageMaker? If
> so, please call for personalized,
> hands-on training."

The first ad brought in two students. That was May of 1990. By November of 1990, I was working

50 hours a week out of my home teaching up to two people at a time in a spare bedroom of our little 1,100 square foot house.

I did computer training for four years. My students referred me to their employers, and I began doing on-site training. Eventually, I began programming databases for companies like Coca-Cola and local manufacturing concerns.

One Thing Leads to Another

Often, you'll get ideas that you feel like you need to follow. You aren't sure where they're leading, but after many days, months or years, you see how those small decisions radically altered the trajectory of your life.

Many times we want God to give us the big pictures – the end objectives. Occasionally, that level of a vision comes to me, but it is more rare than common. Most of the time, I'm just given the next step or the next project.

An example of a project I felt like I should pursue was writing a book on what I'd learned as a computer trainer and consultant. I thought it was a good idea for another revenue stream. In the end, it was a gateway to growth and a different career path. I didn't know that when I set out. I just followed a simple nudge to write a book.

It was 1994 when I wrote that first book: *How to Run a Successful Computer Training Business from Home.* I sold it by uploading excerpts to dial-up bulletin boards, AOL, CompuServe and Prodigy.

That was in the days before the "Web" became popular. People sent me checks in the mail for $24.95, and I mailed them a spiral bound book with a diskette which included course outlines, flyers, brochures, etc. that they could adapt and use as their own.

This was my first experience with revenue that came in without having to swap hours for dollars. It was my first information product.

One of the women who purchased my book became a friend. Alanna Webb lived in Oklahoma and was into desktop publishing. In 1995, she read a magazine article about the Internet. She mentioned she'd like to get into creating web pages. Because Alanna's last name was Webb, I thought it was something she made up! She quickly explained what the Web was. In 1996, we decided to go into business together. Alanna came to Chattanooga, Tennessee where we conducted a mini seminar at a local college. We invited my business clients to come. We taught them about how they could get on the World-Wide Web and how it could help their businesses.

In our business (Pehrson-Webb Group) I did the marketing and customer work and Alanna created the Web sites. She eventually taught me how to do web design. We ended up getting a contract with a big start-up project out of New Jersey. Alanna moved to New Jersey and worked onsite for nearly a year. I worked remotely from home.

When the project ended, Alanna returned to Oklahoma knowing how to program database-driven web sites where the web site visitor could input data that was stored in a database. This was cutting edge for the time. Alanna created a very popular web site for people to input their love stories and poetry.

Eventually in December 1998, I started IdeaMarketers.com to promote experts on various topics. By early 1999, it quickly morphed into the first article directory on the Web. Alanna gave me some programming code she used on her website, and I adapted it to turn IdeaMarketers into a database-driven web site where users could log into their accounts to add and edit articles. Over the years, I adapted the code to create a newsletter builder where people could select articles from the database to create their own newsletters.

IdeaMarketers.com was a writer-publisher matching service. People could use the articles with an author's permission if they included a byline and link to the author's web site.

In the beginning I got a lot of flak from writers who felt I would single-handedly destroy the writing profession and that no one would ever pay for articles again. With IdeaMarketers, anyone could call themselves a writer. But the truth was, if their material wasn't good, it wouldn't get used.

By 2007, IdeaMarketers was one of the most popular authority sites on the Internet. If you wanted exposure and in-bound links to your web site that boosted your search engine positioning, you put articles in IdeaMarketers. The site was written about in many marketing books. The books recommended people use articles to market themselves and load their articles into IdeaMarketers for maximum exposure and inbound links to their web sites.

While *How to Run a Successful Computer Training Business* brought in some cash flow directly, the biggest door it opened for me was meeting Alanna. Had I never met her, I probably wouldn't have been on the cutting edge of web design or online marketing. Without her, I never would have built the first online article directory or met all the people I've learned from over the years. The entire rest of my story would have been radically different had I not written that book!

There are times when the Spirit repeatedly nudges someone to write a book. Most people ignore that and push it aside. They worry that they can't write or that nobody will want to read their book. Or they're worried that there really isn't much money in writing books, so why bother? It's not about the money. It's about whatever doors the Spirit wants to open for you when you write that book. For me, it was about the person I would meet and the entire course of my life. For you it could be something entirely different. If you're feeling the nudge to write a book, I have a course I teach called Spirit-Led Authoring. Details are at www.CreateAWOW.com.

Your Turn

Do you have a thought or an idea that keeps coming to mind? Do you repeatedly push it aside? Maybe you feel it's too hard or impractical. If it keeps coming back, it's probably the Spirit telling you to do that thing. What if you let go of the outcome? What if you didn't worry about it being successful or getting wonderful results or being perfect? What if you just did it and let the Spirit take care of the rest? It could take you somewhere truly magical, but you must act!

Coming Full Circle to the Original Idea

In 2007, I started my Expert Program at IdeaMarketers.com. This gave prominent promotion to experts on various topics. IdeaMarketers experts wrote on everything from Alcoholism to Copywriting to Email Marketing to Homeschooling to Law of Attraction to Tax Lien Investing. I prominently promoted these experts on thousands of articles that related to their expertise – whether those articles were written by them or not.

Each expert got a media room. The media used IdeaMarketers to find guest experts to interview. Our experts reported being found by CNN, TVGuide, Entrepreneur Magazine and other major publications.

Most IdeaMarketers experts were listed first or second in organic Google search and Bing search results because of their exposure on IdeaMarketers.com.

Not until the IdeaMarketers Expert Program was underway for a couple months did I remember, "Hey, this is what I wanted in the beginning when

I started IdeaMarketers – to promote experts! This is where God's been taking me all along!"

Consciously I'd forgotten about the original idea. Most people would say I got side-tracked or that I adapted the site into an article directory. Yet, building the article directory is what gave IdeaMarketers the positioning and traffic necessary to make it a valuable place to promote experts.

Have you ever been somewhere, and a musical piece is playing softly in the background while you're intently focusing on something else? You don't even notice the music, yet you find yourself humming the song later in the day without knowing you are? That's kind of how this idea was for me. I set the music playing and forgot about it, and I found myself "humming" it years later.

I learned from this experience that ideas morph, change, and seem to take on a life of their own if you keep moving with them. In the end, they often seem to come full circle back to the original idea.

The lesson is this: Whenever you have a big idea, you rarely have the resources or ability to achieve it at the onset. If you did, you'd already be doing it. The journey we take helps us accumulate the knowledge, expertise, resources, skillset and contacts we need to make the big idea a reality.

Your Turn

What idea do you have that seems too daunting? That is bigger than you? Have you been tempted to push it aside? Make excuses? Or dodge acting because you don't have all the pieces or don't know how to accomplish every aspect of it? What is one thing you can do today ... even if it's tiny ... that would move you forward toward that thing? Do you know what it is? Okay, then do it!

The Spirit Doesn't Stay Inside a Box

By 2012, IdeaMarketers.com served over 200,000 writers and entrepreneurs. The site brought in five figures a month in ad revenue.

Because of IdeaMarketers' popularity, I became a sought-after guest on podcasts, radio interviews, and telesummits. If I promoted you, you got lots of traffic to your site. I became very well-known in the online marketing and online business world. I put together Amazon bestselling collaborative books which included prominent individuals in the online business world. If I created a collaborative project, I could get just about anyone I wanted to participate.

As someone who loves putting positive messages into the world and highlighting truth and talent, having this level of influence meant a lot to me – and to the people who were part of my projects.

At one point, a businessman, observing what I'd built, said, "I've never seen a business model like yours. It's fascinating."

I thought to myself, "That's because it's not a traditional business model." I built my business step-by-step, with inspiration.

When you tune into inspiration, trust your heart, and act with determination upon inspiration, the Creator of the Universe works through you to create something unique and innovative. What He creates will help a lot more people than just you and your family.

I've observed that God never helps one person when He can help two, ten, hundreds, thousands or millions. The thing is, you often may not really understand what He's building until sometime after you've followed His step-by-step instructions.

One of the biggest myths in business (and life) is that you must create your success like other people are creating theirs. Your definition of success will be different than mine. Our destinations are different, so how can we possibly travel identical roads to different destinations? While certain patterns and principles of goal achievement and success are universal, individual decisions, life experiences and paths will be unique. Tune into inspiration and trust your heart, then act.

Yes, you can learn from other people, but you'll want to trust your heart on what's best for you.

Your Turn

Is there something you feel you should do that other people don't want you to do? Or maybe you think other people wouldn't want you to do it? Or maybe the idea is counter-intuitive or unconventional? If there's something that keeps coming to mind that you feel others would call foolish, it might not be so foolish! Assuming it's moral and ethical and isn't doing physical harm to anyone else, it could be the very thing you're supposed to be doing.

Recognizing The Spirit's Voice

Various terms are used to describe how the Spirit speaks to us. Perhaps that's because the Spirit tends to speak in our own language, in our own way of hearing and understanding. Each of us is unique. Thus, the way we receive divine input is unique to us. Some typical terms or phrases we see used include:

- Trust your heart
- Listen to the still, small voice
- Trust your gut
- Listen to your intuition
- Having a knowing
- Having a feeling
- Receiving a prompting
- Having a vision
- Seeing it in your mind's eye
- Hearing a word or phrase in your mind
- Having a warm feeling
- Having a feeling of peace
- Having a dream
- Strokes of ideas

Learning the Language of the Spirit

Just because I said the Spirit speaks to us in a way we can hear and understand doesn't mean that we automatically hear, understand, and discern the voice of the Spirit. It's like learning a language. It takes time and practice to hear and understand what the Spirit is telling you. I use the word "hear" loosely because for some, it's not auditory at all. It might be visual or sensory in some other way.

One thing that you can bank on is that the Spirit doesn't speak through fear. Even if it's trying to convey a warning, it isn't going to feel like fear. It will perhaps be a feeling that something isn't right. You might even say, "I have a bad feeling about this." Most of the time the Spirit conveys a feeling of peace or a certainty. It could be the certainty that something is right or that it's not right. Just because you have a bad feeling about something doesn't mean you are afraid. If you're operating from fear, that is most likely not the Spirit speaking.

> "God hath not given us the Spirit of fear, but of power and of love and of a sound mind." 2 Timothy 1:7

Another indicator that something is from the Spirit is that it propels you to act. Faith without works is dead. Acting is a key ingredient that shows God you heard and are faithful to the information received. You will receive more inspiration the more you act on what you are given. Act, and act swiftly on what the Spirit reveals. Then it can give you the next step and the next.

Granted, sometimes the action is to simply "Be Still." A feeling of peace is a common way the Spirit speaks to everyone. That feeling of peace could be telling you that the choice you're considering is the right one. Or it could be comforting you and letting you know to just stay put and let things unfold. Often the Spirit simply gives me that feeling of, "It's all going to be okay. Just relax and trust."

I have noticed (as have many others) that once you start developing your ability to discern the Spirit (and the more you act on what it is telling you to do) the more your other senses develop. In this chapter I will share some examples of the various ways the Spirit has spoken with me throughout my life and how my ability to hear and discern have changed over time.

Knowing

As a young woman, the Spirit usually spoke to me as a knowing. I just knew what the truth was, I knew what to do or how to act. It was as if pure knowledge flowed into my mind, and I knew what to do or say as a result of it.

This is still one of the most prominent ways I discern the divine. I have a practice of praying about my day and how to use my time. Almost always an idea strikes, and I know what I am supposed to do that day. When my life was much busier, I'd make a to-do list based on that morning's insight. I wanted to make sure that in all the chaos of mothering and running a business and a household, I did the things the Spirit told me to do for the day.

There was a time when IdeaMarketers.com kept getting hacked. Hackers injected garbage code into tens of thousands of articles. I couldn't figure out how it was happening. I consulted with my hosting provider. He set some of his programmers to work figuring out where the breach was. Weeks went by, but they were not able to figure it out. Finally, I had this idea to look at the logs where it showed every URL that was served to someone from my website.

There were literally millions of lines of code. I remember distinctly being led to a certain section of the logs. There, in one of the URL's was a string of code that was responsible for the hacking. Within perhaps an hour, I programmed code to prevent this type of intrusion from happening again. The hacking stopped.

I absolutely knew the Spirit led me to the right location in the logs. I could have spent years and never found it on my own.

Words or Phrases

A second form of communication that came as I approached my 20's was hearing words in my mind. These instructions come not as thoughts generated by me. They are words injected into my mind as if coming from outside my train of thought. These words stop me in my tracks and grab my attention. They are accompanied by that knowing feeling. An example of this form of spiritual communication is the story I shared earlier. When as a young mother I heard in my mind, "If you go to work outside the home, you'll never come home again," that sentence hit me as a profound truth. It felt so true, I acted in accordance with it. I knew what I had to do (or not do).

Sometimes complete articles or essays are given to me by inspiration. Several years ago, I woke up at 2:00 a.m. with my great aunt's eulogy in my head. As far as I knew she was fine. Yet, her eulogy came to my mind so clearly, that I went to my office, booted my computer, and typed the fully formed eulogy. I went back to bed and called my mother the next morning to ask about my favorite aunt. My mother said that my aunt was in the hospital.

I went to the hospital and had a wonderful visit with her. My aunt died two weeks later, and I gave the eulogy at her funeral. After delivering the eulogy, I sat down and had the most incredible tingly, warm feeling spread all over my body that felt like God gave me a hug. I realized shortly after that this sensation was my aunt giving me a hug. The Spirit knew she was going to pass away and instructed me to write her eulogy. The Spirit told me to call my mother. It led me to my aunt's hospital bed and told me that wonderful feeling I felt was my great aunt giving me a hug.

When we follow the Spirit, it can tell us what our logical minds could never guess. Had I not learned to follow the Spirit, I would have missed this precious opportunity to say goodbye to my aunt and for her to say goodbye to me.

Visuals

Another example of how the Spirit can speak is through flashing a visual into your mind. This has happened many times for me over the years and increasingly in recent years as I work with my clients. A visual will pop into my mind and give me an analogy or a clue for how to explain what I'm seeing at an energetic level.

I'll share with you the first time I recall receiving inspiration in this fashion. My older three children were playing in another room while I was on the computer in the kitchen. We lived in our small 1,100 square foot house so I was never too far away from my kids.

At the time, my daughter Laurel was about 7, Caleb was 5, and Joshua was 3. Laurel and Caleb came to me in the kitchen and Caleb said, "Mom, Josh is dead."

"What?"

"No, he's not. He's just sleeping," Laurel said.

"No," Caleb repeated with urgency, "He's dead."

I ran down the hall to the first room on the left. The seat cushion was not on the recliner and the recliner was stretched all the way back with Joshua's little body lying on it. He was lifeless and pale.

"What happened?" I exclaimed as I rushed to him and scooped up his body to carry it into the bedroom where my husband was sleeping. I woke up my husband and put Joshua on the bed.

As we worked to resuscitate Joshua, a visual flashed into my mind of Caleb and Joshua as teenagers with ball caps on. They were perhaps 14 and 16 years old, walking down the hall, healthy and just fine. A feeling of peace swept over me and I knew Joshua would be okay.

Within moments, Joshua revived, and the kids explained that they had been playing choo-choo train on the recliner. Joshua was sitting furthest back against the recliner back, then they put a pillow in front of him and the next child leaned against that pillow. Then they put a pillow in front of the second child, while the third leaned against that pillow. In other words, they made a child pillow sandwich and Joshua, being in the back, became asphyxiated.

After a trip to the hospital to have him checked for good measure, we got rid of that recliner, and Joshua grew up. He's now a father with his own children.

The visual that flashed into my mind gave me peace in a terrifying moment. It also served me over the years. I knew those two boys would make it at least through their teenage years.

Meditative Visualization

In recent years, an increasing number of people have tapped into the power of visualization. What used to be considered "daydreaming" is now a viable method for accelerating toward your goals and aspirations. If you can't see yourself doing it, frankly, you won't do it. So, we have vision boards, and we spend time using our imagination to see and feel what it's going to be like when we achieve our dreams.

There is another power to visualization which I've found surpasses this. It taps into a power far beyond our own. I first learned about it in 2009 when I met a woman named Judy Rankin. Judy is an energy intuitive who uses guided meditations and what she calls "enscripts" to read people's energy. Each of her enscripts is as unique as the individual. In fact, they're even more unique because I've received several of these enscripts and no two are the same. I've found them to be a wonderful symbolic depiction of who I am, where I'm heading next, and what heavenly resources are available to me.

The first enscript Judy led me on was a guided meditation to the Savior. It was so real that I felt as if I had visited with Him, felt His love for me, and given Him all my cares. It was so moving, there were tears streaming down my face. This meditation and a few that followed taught me that I could take these visual journeys myself. I could visit with the Savior in my heart, mind and spirit. I could converse with Him like one person converses with another. Since that time, I've visited with Him many times.

Sometimes we have long, insightful conversations where I come away with the direction I need to take next. Sometimes the insights are so powerful, I know I could never have discovered them on my own. Other times, when I'm very troubled, all I can manage to do is go sit with Him and put my head on His chest. After some time there, everything feels better.

It's such an incredible peace simply sitting with Him.

Other times He takes me to different parts of the world or even to remote regions of the universe. We've walked on the beaches of Monterey, California, stood by tall Irish cliffs, visited the desert, gone to Hawaii and flown to the cradle of creation — a vast nebula at the center of the universe. Wherever He takes me, His creations illustrate His awesome power, majesty and love. There is NOTHING that is too hard for Him. Nothing that is too overwhelming. Not only have I found solace and forgiveness in handing Him my pride, my disappointments and my mistakes; but also, I've felt incredible joy in giving Him my hopes, dreams and aspirations.

I don't claim to be a prophetess or to have literally seen my Savior face-to-face, but He does feel incredibly real to me. Whether you want to call it simply my wishful imagination, a prayer, a meditation, or my spirit communing with His, it yields wonderful benefits. I feel more joy, peace, clarity, inspiration and love. He can drive away my darkest doubts, my greatest fears, and severest worries. I don't know of any form of visualization that can top that!

How Does It Work?

I'll share with you a process that might help you train yourself to commune with Him. This is just my method. So, feel free to adapt it until you find what works for you.

Use a soundtrack. I have a specific playlist of music on my MP3 player that I use to help me relax and find a calmer, more reflective state. I use a lot of Brian Crain piano music. Yiruma is good too. Listen, breathe deep and relax.

Start with a prayer and a very specific request. The more specific I can be, the better. I may be looking for specific help in my business. I might be feeling overwhelmed and need clarity and peace. I might be concerned about one of my children. (Hint: you can take other people to Jesus in your mind! I've seen miracles happen with this.)

Have a routine for entering the Lord's presence. After the prayer closes, I have a specific way I approach the Lord and enter His presence. It's just a "routine" that is personal to me. Find your own way of finding Him in your mind. It could be something like traveling across a bridge, passing through a curtain, or walking through a door.

Once you've entered His presence, ask Him your question, or tell Him what you want to feel or know. Be still and listen to Him. He may ask you questions. Many times, my sessions with the Savior are a lot like a "coaching visit" where He pulls the answers out of me.

Devote the time. I've spent an hour or two in this place. When I absolutely must go about my day, but the encounter has been so wonderful that I don't want to leave, I'll ask Him to come along with me throughout my day. I continue to walk and talk with Him in my mind as if He is right there beside me as I clean the house or work.

Don't get frustrated if sometimes you don't communicate as clearly. There are lots of times that the best I can do is find Him, put my head on His shoulder and let Him hug me. Be there with Him and accept what comes.

There you have my secret to visualizing. Spend a little time in the morning traveling to solar systems, nebulae, and the Milky Way with the Savior, and when you come back to your life, the goals you thought looked so insurmountable and overwhelming will seem peacefully do-able.

Keep a Journal

However your answers come, be sure to journal them. I often write down my dreams that feel particularly meaningful. Sometimes, I have dreams that guide me, help me figure out what's going on in my life, and even warn me of what may lie ahead. It's a good idea to journal your dreams. In fact, I recommend keeping a journal of all the inspiration you receive regardless of the form it takes.

During the most difficult times of my life, I have received the most inspiration. For example, going through a divorce after 28 years of marriage was a big decision for me to make. Through it all, God helped me make decisions and navigate the process. He even showed me what was coming in my future. I kept a journal throughout this process. Many of the things God showed me through meditation (and that I recorded) literally came to pass.

In fact, the life I have now with my husband Dave was shown to me years in advance. I have the uncanny journal entries to prove it. I talk more about that story in *Confidence Rising!*

The great thing about keeping a journal of your inspiration is that you begin to see a pattern in how God speaks to you. You also have a record to go back to when amnesia sets in. After a lifetime of seeking God's direction, I've learned that He loves to reveal to us who we are and what we're here to do. Yet, the human tendency is to forget those moments of revelation or to doubt them. We forget who God told us we are and what we're here to do. If you've kept a good journal and recorded those insights when they come, you can go back to your journal. If you've forgotten who you are, your journal will help you remember. You'll also remember the goodness of God and His miracles in your life.

Your Turn

How does the Spirit speak to you? Review the list I gave you at the beginning of this chapter. Which of these have you experienced? Or perhaps you have another way of receiving inspiration that I did not mention. Take a moment to journal about times when you have experienced one or more methods of receiving personal revelation. Make it a practice of recording your moments of insight.

God's Bread Trails

I don't know that God works this way with everyone, but with me, He leads me along bread trails. This is especially the case if I have a burning question or a need for greater understanding. If I am seeking guidance or answers to a perplexing question, I receive a series of little insights or levels of understanding or knowledge that build on one another. Out of a deep desire, I am gradually led to an answer.

Where there is a question, there is an answer. By law, it is the case. If you have a question, God has an answer, and He's willing to share that answer with you. He rarely gives it all in one big download. He doesn't usually plop a fully formed answer directly into my lap. Sometimes that happens, but on bigger things, He tends to send me on a scavenger hunt. I don't know whether this is because He knows that we only value what we put some effort into or whether it's like being in a dark room and gradually turning up the lights. When you've been in a dark room asleep and someone flips the light on, it's blinding. But when they gradually turn up the lights, your eyes can adjust to it. Perhaps God is helping us gradually adjust to a new level of truth by sending us on a bread trail to discover it.

What do the bread pieces look like? Maybe you're sitting in church and someone says something that feels significant. You want to write it down. Or maybe your eyes tear up a bit or you feel what has been said is important. I've had this happen sometimes when I don't even know why what the person said is so important. I just feel it in my soul that it's significant to me, and I'll jot it down. Anytime you feel those types of impressions, write them down. It could be part of your bread trail.

Sometimes insights will come in dreams. Or a friend will say something, or I'll have an opportunity to learn something new. I pay attention when something keeps showing up. For example, without telling anyone about a business problem I was trying to figure out, two different people recommended the same piece of software on the same day. I took that as a clue that I needed to check out that software. Sure enough, it was a great solution to my problem.

As you pick up the pieces, they are rarely the full answer. As you run with a piece to the puzzle, you'll encounter another piece and another. The trick to the bread trail is you've got to move your feet. You pick up the first insight and act on it while keeping an eye out for the next piece. If the next piece suggests you move in another direction, move that way. Keep following all the pieces that come up, and eventually you will be led to a fully formed solution. Eventually, you'll have this "aha moment" where you exclaim, "Oh, I get it now! This is it!"

The trick is to ask specifically and then keep your eyes open. Expect the nuggets of inspiration or insight to come. They can come from anywhere over the course of days, weeks, months or even years. Start collecting them. Sometimes I'll get a white board, write the insights on sticky notes and keep putting them up until I get the full picture.

Sometimes the pieces will come when you're doing something completely different, just going about your life. Let the pieces simmer like a stew while you do things like wash dishes, work in the yard, or paint your house. Often, for me, it takes getting out of my head and doing something physical to get the next insight or for everything to coalesce.

Everyone's minds work differently, and the Spirit speaks to us differently, but I've found that many people can relate to the bread trail analogy.

Your Turn

Can you relate to the God's Bread Trail analogy? How and when have you been led from one insight or truth to another until you gained full understanding of a concept or answer to a personal question? How will you start paying better attention to God's bread trails in your life? Will you use a white board? A journal? A special section of notes in your phone? Carry a little notebook with you?

Being Yourself

"Find out who you are and do it on purpose."
– Dolly Parton

I'm a big believer in the value of personality theory. There are various personality theories out there – like the Meyers-Briggs and Disc Profile. One of my dearest friends (Lisa Rae Preston – you'll see her name again later) has a Masters in personality theory. Over the years she's taught me much about people and how they tick. I've used what Lisa taught me in team building, collaborations, communicating with my kids and clients, and interacting with the various people I meet.

My first introduction to personality theory was back in the late 90's when a coach had me take the DISC Profile®.

D – dominance, drive, direct
I – influence, influential
S – steadiness, stability
C – conscientious, compliant, careful, cautious, calculating

My results showed that my natural strengths were Influence and Steadiness. My lowest area was Conscientiousness.

My adaptive score showed that my Conscientiousness had adapted to be my strongest area when normally it was my weakest. When I took the test, I didn't have a clue what my scores meant.

A friend, who had worked with an expert in personality theory, asked her former employer what my scores meant. He said, "Marnie would be happiest working with people, motivating and inspiring them, but because she needs to make money, she's taken up computer work and adapted until her critical thinking scores are inflated."

My scores meant that my spirit wanted to make a positive impact in the world, but my logical mind (given my circumstances) felt tech work was a safer place to earn a living.

When this man analyzed my assessment scores, I realized I really would be happier inspiring people. That sounded like a completely delicious idea. At the time I was a computer trainer and programmer. I had only written the one computer business book and hadn't gotten into any of the emotional work I do now with people.

I was good at what I did. I enjoyed it, but I spent way too much time working and too little time enjoying my life and my children. Much of the time I was like a workhorse with blinders on, focusing on the tasks at hand, and not stopping to truly enjoy the blessings I had.

When I understood the results of my DISC Profile®, I determined that one day I would shift what I was doing so that I was doing less of the tech work and more influencing people for good.

Gradually, over time, my work shifted. I went from being a computer trainer, programmer and consultant to speaking, teaching and writing. Starting in 2000, I began writing inspirational articles and books. By 2010, I actively had a side-line work where I was speaking, teaching and writing about how each of us can work together to light the world and make it a better place.

I don't regret my years of tech work. It's been invaluable to me. I can get things out online quickly because I have all the tech skills to build a website, use social media and email platforms, create online courses, publish books and more. I don't have to hire or wait on someone else to do things. I can get them done myself – fast!

Nothing is ever wasted when you let the Spirit lead the way.

When You're Emotionally Numb

Have you ever gone through a set of circumstances and gotten to the point where you were emotionally numb? Did it feel safer to shut off your emotions than deal with them?

That's where I was for many years. Although tech work paid the bills and took care of my family, it was — as many jobs are — emotionally and spirituality dissatisfying, and even draining. I've had to process and release a lot of "Mom-guilt" for all the years my children spent entertaining themselves in the next room while I sat at a computer working long hours to make ends meet. I've had to apologize and forgive myself for the times I lost my temper and yelled too much or disciplined too harshly.

Because I'd adapted my life to do work that was not my natural place of joy, I had to shut off many emotions. I didn't have time for the distraction of temperamental emotions – mine or anyone else's. So, I stuffed a lot of emotions and ignored many aspects of my intuition. I also didn't give my children the emotional support they needed. I was too busy trying to tread water from day to day.

Over the years, as I began to do more of what brought me joy and less of what didn't, I noticed a change in myself and how I interacted with my children. The more in-touch I became with my emotions and the more I did what brought me joy, the less stressed I felt. The less stress I experienced in my work, the more attentive and patient I became with my children.

I have six children – girl, boy, boy, and then girl, boy, boy. I often say God gave me a do-over. I was a much better mother with the last three children than I was with the first three. That is largely because I nestled into who I am and what God put me on this earth to do. I stopped trying to be my mother. I couldn't use her authoritative disciplinary style effectively. I began to process my emotions better and did more of the work I'm naturally created to do. All of this lowered my stress levels, brought more joy into my days, and thus led to me being a much better mother.

One pivotal moment came for me at about the turn of the century. A coach I was working with trained me to put self-care on my to-do list. She recommended I congratulate myself in doing self-care activities as if I'd accomplished a major task. I don't know about you, but I love checking things off a to-do list. With self-care activities on my to-do list, I could check them off and feel good about it. Ever since I started doing that, I've never felt the least bit of guilt about self-care.

Another thing that created a huge improvement in my emotional intelligence was working with a couple of SimplyHealed™ practitioners. They helped me release a lot of the emotions I'd been stuffing for years. When the opportunity came to get certified in SimplyHealed™ myself, I jumped at the chance. One of the first things I learned as a SimplyHealed™ Practitioner was how to identify and recognize my emotions and process them swiftly so I could move to a more liberated state. Energy work also helped me distinguish my thoughts and feelings from other people's thoughts and feelings. When you're a mom taking responsibility for everyone's happiness (which is impossible to ensure), the pressure you put on yourself is intense. I eventually learned that I am not responsible for my spouse's or children's emotions. Their stories, perspectives, experiences and emotions are theirs. It's not my job to own their stuff or fix it. I can be supportive, encouraging and loving, but their stuff isn't about me. It's about them.

When I finally got this, my relationships began to improve and so did my ability to communicate respectfully and with greater patience and understanding.

If you are stuffing your emotions or numbing yourself, you're also numbing your ability to hear the still small voice of the Spirit.

Your Turn

Is there any area of your life in which you are not allowing yourself to feel? Are you stuffing down pain? Are you allowing yourself to experience happiness and joy? Are you experiencing bliss moments regularly? Or are you going through the motions? What action will you take to open yourself to a full range of emotions and allow yourself to feel more? Are you owning other people's stuff? How will you acknowledge that and release it?

Karol Truman wrote a book called Feelings Buried Alive Never Die. The feelings we stuff end up showing up in our bodies... in illness, disease, self-sabotage, etc. You don't want that! Do you need to get help with processing your emotions? Don't be afraid to ask for help! Nearly every client I work with has some emotion they haven't adequately processed and that they are able to release in our time together. It's incredibly common, and there is help available.

Letting Go of the Outcome

One of the biggest obstacles I needed to overcome was a fear of consulting. At least that's what I thought it was. Really it was a fear of failure. I didn't mind consulting on tech subjects, but when it came to consulting people on what to do to move their businesses forward, I had trouble. There were so many times when I knew what the person needed to do. I'd give them advice, but I also intuitively sensed that they would not follow through. They had too many fears, too many limiting beliefs, too much past baggage to move forward. I felt bad taking a client's money for business consulting when I knew they wouldn't follow through. I stopped offering consulting services for a while. I couldn't feel good about it. I was afraid of a client's failure because I interpreted that as my failing.

After becoming a SimplyHealed™ Practitioner I learned first and foremost to let go of the outcome. You can't shift energy if you're obsessed over whether it shifts or not. You tell the energy to move and then trust that it moves as directed.

You can't be a good consultant if you think it's all your responsibility to bring the results. The person has a responsibility to themselves to move forward and act on any advice given. There are two individuals in a consulting situation. Each person must carry their own weight.

I could give business advice, but if the person didn't follow it, that was their choice. I didn't need to feel guilty taking their money for doing my part of the job just because they didn't follow through on their part.

Your Turn

What fear is keeping you from doing what you enjoy? Are you taking too much responsibility for the outcome? I love the phrase, "What God originates, He orchestrates." I don't know who originally said it, but it is incredibly true. We worry way too much about having to control outcomes. When we let go of the outcome and get out of the way, the Spirit can orchestrate things for us and take care of the details. We just need to act when the Spirit inspires. What outcomes are you worrying about? How is this stopping your progress? What if you gave the details to God? What would that look like for you?

Get Rid of the Clutter to Move Forward

The second thing SimplyHealed™ gave me was a way to move typical fears, doubts and limiting beliefs people faced out of the way so they could move forward. I had always intuitively sensed if a person had baggage blocking their path to success. It was as though they had cans and bags and boxes of garbage blocking their pathway. Not until I became a SimplyHealed™ Practitioner did I know how to help them move those blockages so they could get on with what they are here to do.

Now I'm able to combine energy work with my business consulting to assist clients in moving forward more effectively. I'm not just telling them what to do and then leaving them with their hang-ups in the way. We energetically move the baggage out of the way and connect the person to the outcome they want. Then I give them a musical piece that reinforces the positive emotions and outcomes.

I use music, nature, creativity and energy therapy to bring people hope, direction and inspiration so they can be their highest, best, and most authentic selves. I like to think that I teach and show people how to invite the Spirit into their lives so they can be more than they could be on their own. All of us can do miraculous things with the Spirit flowing through us.

If there are limiting beliefs, old traumas, confusion, fears, or areas where we're out of integrity, it's harder for the Spirit to work through us. If we get those blockages cleared away, the Spirit can flow through unobstructed. We can help spread more light into the world. We can be a greater influence for good on the people within our sphere of influence. If the world needs anything today, it needs more light, more love and more goodness.

The more talented people there are who tune into the Spirit, the better the world will be.

Your Turn

Learn a bit about yourself by taking a personality test. As I mentioned earlier, the DISC test helped me make a shift in my work overtime. The Meyers-Briggs has taught me to understand myself, my strengths and how to better interact with others. Discover your strengths and your weaknesses. You don't have to be someone you're not. Find other people to bring onto your team who make up for your weak areas while you do what you do best and what brings you the most joy.

As Dolly Parton said, "Find out who you are and do it on purpose!" You don't have to do it overnight. You can do it over time ... like I did. Gradually integrate more of what brings the greatest joy into your life.

Follow Your Bliss and Expect the Best

Joseph Campbell said:

> "If you follow your bliss you put yourself on a kind of track that has been there all the while, waiting for you, and the life that you ought to be living is the one you are living. When you can see that, you begin to meet people who are in your field of bliss, and they open doors to you. I say, follow your bliss and don't be afraid, and doors will open where you didn't know they were going to be."

Joseph Campbell didn't say follow what makes you aggravated. He didn't say, "Expect the worst" or "Expect people to do you dirty." (That's Southern slang for treating you unjustly.) No, he said, "Follow your bliss!" Expect people and opportunities to come out of nowhere to work together for your good and your blessing. This is something I've tried to do over the years – do the things that bring me the greatest happiness daily and expect the best.

By following my bliss in small things, I've been able to transform my life so that most of my day-to-day activities are things that I truly enjoy.

Especially during the more hectic seasons of my life, I've found it helpful to take mini "bliss breaks" throughout the day that keep me focused on the positive and beautiful in the world. Some things I do are:

- Go outside for a few minutes and dig in my garden or go for a walk
- Sit on my front porch and count my blessings
- Take a walk to pet the horses
- Take a snuggly power nap with my husband
- Go to lunch with a friend
- Work out
- Drive "top down, tunes up" through the countryside
- Crank up my music and sing along
- Take a break and chat about something meaningful with my husband
- Play the piano
- Kick back with a good book.

I've found that sprinkling these "bliss breaks" throughout the day not only makes me feel better and more grateful for what I have, but also brings more good things to me.

I challenge you to make a list of what brings you bliss and start the habit. Ask yourself, "What brings me happiness? What brings me true joy?" Sprinkle your bliss breaks throughout the day and watch wonderful things unfold in your life. While you're at it, think bigger! Point your entire life and focus toward what brings you bliss. It's a miraculous way to live!

"Whatsoever things are true, whatsoever things are honest, whatsoever things are just, whatsoever things are pure, whatsoever things are lovely, whatsoever things are of good report; if there be any virtue, and if there be any praise, think on these things." (The New Testament, Philippians 4:8)

Your Turn

Make your own Bliss List. Create a list of things that rejuvenate you that you can do in 10-15-minute breaks throughout the day. Keep that list handy. Make sure you integrate 3-6 of these throughout your day. The more you can integrate bliss, the more your entire life becomes blissful.

Valuing Yourself

If I've struggled with anything over my 30 years in business, it's been valuing myself. I'm notoriously affordable. I often don't see my value. I think "Oh, anyone can do this." And then I cheapen myself and price myself accordingly.

For example: Back in the early '90s, when I first branched out into doing more than computer training, I did some graphic design and desktop publishing. One of my clients ran a business that sold mechanical parts. He had a catalog with line-drawings of various tools and mechanical gizmos (I have no idea what those things were). He would have me scan line drawings of existing mechanical parts and then use a graphics program to adapt them per his specifications. He'd sit beside me and say, "Okay, erase the right end of that and draw a circle on it." Or some other such thing. Step-by-step, he'd sit beside me and have me draw these intricate tools per his instruction. It was tedious, but he was very nice, friendly and incredibly complimentary of my work.

He bragged on me all the time about my skills. He paid me $10 an hour. At the same time, I was making $30 an hour doing programming for a manufacturing company. I got more like $20 for training. He paid me the least of any of my clients.

Finally, I realized, "Yes, he's a nice man, but I need money more than I need praise. And I really don't enjoy the tedium of this work." Prayerfully, I considered what to do, and I felt very strongly that I needed to raise my rates across the board to $40 an hour. I crafted a letter and mailed it to all my clients explaining the rate increase and when it would go into effect.

The man who was paying me $10 an hour, couldn't afford to pay me $40. So, I stopped working for him. The manufacturing company (who also loved me and my work) gladly gave me $40 an hour and continued to hire me for more work.

Ironically, I enjoyed the database work I did for the manufacturing company much more than the tedious graphics work that frequently gave me headaches.

Periodically, I review what I'm doing in my work. Which aspects do I enjoy most? Which activities leave me stressed? For example, where I am today, tedious tech work gives me a headache. I'd much rather create music and make a book trailer for an author client. Even better, I'd rather have the pure joy of conducting a SimplyHealed™ session with a client who comes away feeling unburdened, de-stressed and knowing what next steps to take in their life or business. Those things make me feel like I am fulfilling my purpose and making a difference in the world.

Not always, but many times the people who are paying the least are the most work and causing the most stress. It's the 80-20 rule. Eighty percent of your income comes from twenty percent of your clients. Twenty percent of your clients are the ones that cause 80% of your stress.

After evaluating my life and identifying the things that are stressing me, I usually find things I'm just tolerating. I either fix those tolerations, delegate them to someone else, automate the processes, or drop them.

Your Turn

Take time to make a list of all the things you are doing in your life and in your business. Rate them on a scale of 1-5 (1 being the least enjoyable and 5 being the most). Look at the activities with the lowest scores. Which of these can you eliminate or drop? Which can you delegate?

As you go through your life, you might ask yourself, "How does this work, or this project, or this activity, make me feel?" And then work toward doing what makes you incredibly joyful and brings you peace and satisfaction.

No Amount of Money Is Worth It

One thing I learned early is that no amount of money will make me take on some clients. I'm not saying they're bad people. They just aren't a match for me.

For example, I don't work well with people who micromanage my work. I love working with clients who appreciate and value my innovation and creativity and give me lots of space to explore how I can serve them and deliver the results they seek. If someone wants to micromanage every little thing I do, I'm not a fan. It stresses me out. I feel like someone has clipped my wings. My freedom and sanity are worth more than all the money in the world.

I've also learned not to work with people who have nothing nice to say about their previous employees or subcontractors. In the beginning, I listened to a prospect's complaints about previous subcontractors and took them on as a challenge. It was an opportunity to prove I could deliver and do a better job. I swiftly learned this was a huge mistake. People who look for problems will find them – no matter how good of a job you do. You'll be the person they're complaining about next. Either that or you'll work and stress yourself to death jumping through their hoops.

I now take complaints as a major red flag. I steer clear of working for those people. No matter how badly you need the money or how much you think you'd like the project, run if someone is complaining and moaning about former employees or subcontractors.

Your Turn

Think of the clients or customers you have. Do you have certain clients who are draining you? Who (if anyone) isn't a good match for you? What can you do about that? Can you delegate their account to someone else on your team? Can you refer them to a colleague who is a better match?

Beware of Charismatic Visionaries

Another truth I've learned in my 30 years is: Trust your instincts. If your gut says there's something off, then there is something off. Trust it. I don't recall having a gut feeling that there was something off at the beginning of the story I'm about to share, but I knew to run by the end.

In the late 1990's, I was hired as a marketing consultant by a charismatic and visionary businessman. He was very complimentary of my work. For my part I enjoyed taking his big ideas and crafting marketing proposals and joint venture partnership proposals. He was putting together some innovative collaborations with cutting-edge online technology. He also paid me incredibly well.

What I didn't realize was that this man wasn't ethical. For example, he conned one of my co-subcontractors into mortgaging her house to invest in the project. When it went south, she lost it all. Later, this woman and I and every other subcontractor on the project ended up getting sued by one of the companies involved.

All of us subcontractors went together and got a lawyer to handle our cases. Fortunately, the suit was dropped against all of us. I considered myself lucky to have come out of the situation with only $500 in legal fees. After the dust settled, this man came back to me, having reincorporated under a new name, wanting me to work with him again.

Yeah, right, no way.

I'll be honest, I don't recall my gut warning me about this man or his motives. I didn't see it coming. But I learned a valuable lesson that taught me about the nature of some people. This lesson has stuck with me over the years and has helped me avoid situations where I could have gotten involved with similar individuals. Because of this first situation, I learned to recognize these types of people and steer clear of them.

Some years later, I was invited to be a part of another big visionary project by a very charismatic individual who had lots of influential people involved. I did a little with it for a time. The leader wanted me to volunteer more of my time to the project. This person was convinced if I did volunteer now, the pay-outs later would be substantial.

I never got a good feeling about it. It wasn't that I felt this charismatic visionary wasn't sincere or didn't really intend to build what they said they would. I don't believe the person had sinister motives. I just didn't feel right about investing my time and energy in the project. So, I politely refused. (A side note about valuing yourself: Any time someone asks you to volunteer because the payouts later will be huge, and you do that, you're not valuing yourself! My volunteer work is done for free because I believe in the cause, the project, and the potential result, NOT because I'm expecting a big payout later!)

About five years later I heard from a friend (who did get involved) that things went south. Money was mismanaged, ill-appropriated and some illegal things done by one of the players. This made everyone involved look bad.

While I don't think the charismatic visionary set out to misappropriate and mismanage funds, I've learned that charismatic visionaries simply don't have an eye for details. They take imprudent shortcuts to get their ideas to market faster. They're overly zealous. They've usually gathered a bunch of people together on something, and they want to look big and successful to keep the excitement going. Thus, they toss money around too soon and don't pay attention to details – like reporting, bookkeeping, regulations, taxes, etc. This makes them prime targets for dishonest companies and individuals to slip in and do things that wreck the whole ship.

I'm not saying all charismatic visionaries can't be trusted. Just make sure they have people on board that keep them in check and make up for their lack of vision on the day-to-day details.

Above all, trust your gut! If it says, "This looks too good to be true." Or "Don't get involved," don't!

Your Turn

Think back through your life. Think of times when you had a bad feeling about something, you moved ahead, and it turned out badly. Think of the times when a single thought entered your mind as a warning or as a precaution to take and you ignored it and things didn't turn out well. Is there anything currently in your life that feels like it's off? Determine how you will start listening to these warning signals and adjusting your course accordingly.

What if You're the Charismatic Visionary?

Maybe you see a bit of yourself in the charismatic visionary. Do you have lots of big ideas and an ability to rally people on board your team? If you find it exhilarating to make gutsy moves, be aware that you do have blind spots. You need to surround yourself with highly ethical watchdog types of people who will make sure that everything you do is above board. They should keep an eye on all your bookkeeping systems and accounting and make sure everything in your business is handled properly, honestly and ethically.

Find someone with an exceptional sense of discernment who can warn you if someone you've brought on board has the potential to be unethical. My father could be a charismatic visionary. He was known for his "money making schemes" (or so my mother called them). My mother had watchdog discernment. In his enthusiasm to implement his big ideas, my dad often got involved with individuals who took advantage of his enthusiasm and trusting nature. My mother warned him not to do business with certain people. The times he ignored my mother's warnings were the times someone took advantage of his trusting nature. Those times when he listened to her, he kept out of trouble.

You may feel like the detailed watchdog types put a damper on your enthusiasm, but you need these people to protect your interests and the interests of everyone else on your project.

Avoid the temptation to take shortcuts, to make outlandish promises, or to borrow more than you can repay. If you're banking on your ship coming in to pay things back, you're treading on thin ice. All these behaviors will get you in trouble. I have news for you, most ships don't come in. Can you pay these people back if those ships sink?

Some businesspeople view bankruptcy as a solution. I don't believe that's ethical. In fact, I think that saying you'll just file bankruptcy if it doesn't work out is wrong. It's theft. It's one thing if life deals you a series of blows and, after all you can do, you must reluctantly file bankruptcy. It's quite another to take unwise risks and have bankruptcy as your backup plan.

What We Obtain Too Cheap, We Esteem Too Lightly

"What we obtain too cheap, we esteem too lightly: It is dearness only that gives everything its value. Heaven knows how to put a proper price upon its goods; and it would be strange indeed if so celestial an article as freedom should not be highly rated." – Thomas Paine, The American Crisis

When you undervalue what you do or what you offer, others will undervalue it. If you highly value what you do (and offer a valuable service), other people will highly value it. There are those in the business industry who charge exhorbitant prices and don't deliver. I cringe when someone tells me they shelled out thousands of dollars for some scam internet service that made outlandish promises for how much money customers would make if they purchased their product or service. Then, the customer received absolutely nothing of value.

When I say you should highly value yourself, I'm talking about highly valuing what you do that has high value. When you do a job well, when you have years of expertise and wisdom to share, when you have a solution to a challenging problem that a segment of society struggles with, value it.

If you don't value it, no one else will. When you've put together something unique and valuable, if you price it too cheaply, people will think it's not worth much. They won't take it seriously. They may buy it, but they'll probably set your product on a shelf and never utilize it.

Years ago, I invested $1,500 in a specialized training. I had the money for it, but I didn't toss around $1,500 for training lightly. Because I invested in that training, I valued it more than if I'd paid $150 for it. I followed through. I put the knowledge I gained from that training to work.

As a result, I've recouped my investment many times over.

There is more than one way to invest. It's not always about money. Investing your time, energy, influence, freedom and other resources is also an investment.

If you're money-poor, invest your time or your energy.

Back in 2000, I was going through a difficult period financially. We'd been hit by some unexpected expenses, and I was struggling to forgive the person who caused them. At the time I was writing a weekly column on SheLovesGod.com (my Christian women's site) and wrote about what I was learning about forgiveness.

Out of the blue, a woman contacted me asking questions about the article. She asked if she could share her story with me and get my advice. I agreed, and she shared that she'd been through a difficult situation and was struggling to forgive someone.

After hearing her story, I emailed back, "Wow, that's a doozy! I guess you may have guessed, I'm struggling to forgive someone too and that's why I wrote the article."

She hadn't guessed and asked me to share my story. I did not want to share my story with this person. I didn't really know her, and I felt weird sharing such a personal financial challenge. I read her email and then got up from my computer and went to the kitchen to make dinner.

As I stood over the stove, praying in my mind about whether I should share my situation with this stranger, I felt strongly that I should. She'd been very open and vulnerable. I felt I could trust her with my story. (Note: This is the other side of the "Trust your gut!" concept.)

After dinner, I emailed her back with my situation. Her response was something like, "Oh, financial challenges. I can help you with that!"

She proceeded to tell me that she had recently been certified as a Bob Proctor Facilitator. She too had struggled financially in the past and had found information that transformed her life. She and her husband had seen great results by applying these laws of thought.

This woman, Leslie Householder, is now one of my dearest friends. Over the next few months, Leslie shared the principles of thought that govern prosperity. We emailed back and forth; she generously priority mailed me a complete VHS set of Bob Proctor's Born Rich program, as well as audio cassettes of his version of the 1910 Wallace D. Wattle's classic, The Science of Getting Rich.

Because I'd studied self-help materials before and never seen any significant results, I was skeptical. I kept wanting to take what she taught me back to Scripture to see if it held water. Fortunately, Leslie came from the same Christian faith I did and was able to speak my language. Together we found scriptural backup for these laws.

By implementing the laws, I swiftly doubled my income. I was impressed! At the time, I was doing a yearly SheLovesGod Virtual Women's Conference. I asked Leslie if she'd be a presenter at my next conference. She agreed to. I asked if she had a web site. She did not. I built her one and showed her how to maintain it.

I encouraged her to take our conversations and turn them into a book. She wrote *Hidden Treasures: Heaven's Astonishing Help with Your Money Matters.* I pointed her in the direction of how to get her book in print. Later, when I got into writing fiction, I encouraged her to write *The Jackrabbit Factor.*

The physical products and personal coaching and mentoring I received from Leslie Householder (and have continued to receive as her friend over the years) have a street price of hundreds of thousands of dollars. In fact, for me they are priceless. Using what she taught me, I went on to make seven times the annual income I was making when I met her.

I didn't have thousands of dollars to give Leslie when she generously taught me the principles. Fortunately, something inside Leslie told her to "help this woman" and she followed the Spirit's recommendation. Because she was willing to invest in me, I was able to expedite the process that, in turn, enabled Leslie to impact tens of thousands of lives for good.

Over the years I have continued to sing Leslie Householder's praises and promote her prominently. I love when heaven facilitates these symbiotic relationships. Money may never change hands, but the impact is exponential for both parties.

Psychic Income

You may be thinking: "Wait! You just gave her advice for free. Aren't you undervaluing yourself?" There is such a thing as "psychic income." Perhaps for a time, I needed my $10 an hour graphic client's praise. But eventually, I no longer needed it that badly.

There have been other times I've gladly done work for people at a reduced rate or even for free because I felt prompted to do so (just like Leslie was prompted to help me). In those situations, I've had the "psychic income" of knowing that I was doing something that God wanted me to do. Through repeated experience, I know that God pays handsomely – more bounteously than money alone.

There have been times when I've been talking with someone and learn (or have a feeling) that they have a unique talent, gift, expertise or message. I've had the Spirit tell me, "Help this person." I made a policy that when that happens, I do so, no-questions-asked and no fee required.

In the upcoming section on Quantum Collaboration, I'll share some powerful examples of what I mean by psychic income and how helping those you feel prompted by the Spirit to help can lead to incredible results.

Your Turn

Has there ever been a time you felt prompted to help someone and you did? What was the psychic income that came from that experience? Did you

walk lighter through the day? Feel more
connected to the Divine? Or do you have a story
like mine and Leslie's that turned out to be a
symbiotic friendship?

What's Your Pivot Point?

My friend Phillip Davis of Tungsten Branding, who was the naming and branding expert for IdeaMarketers, taught me something important a long time ago. He taught me about finding your pivot point in business.

Are you familiar with basketball and your pivot foot? As a 5'10" female in the 1980's I played a lot of basketball. In that sport, if you aren't dribbling the ball, you can plant one foot in a stationary location and pivot your body 360 degrees, stepping with your other foot. Using this method, you can keep the ball away from opponents until you decide what you want to do with it. Knowing how to pivot is a powerful tool in basketball. If you use it with confidence, your opponents will keep their distance, you'll have freedom of movement, you will have time to think straight and see clearly what you want to do next. Then, even with all the noise, pressure and confusion going on around you, you can execute what you want to do with confidence and skill.

In business, if you know your pivot point, it gives you the freedom and range of motion to explore possibilities in your business, yet keeps you grounded and centered on what you do best.

For example, Phil Davis told me about a tuxedo shop owner he knew in Brevard, North Carolina. Phil attended the local Chamber of Commerce with the man. The man's shop struggled when prom and wedding seasons were over. Phil suggested the man not think of himself as someone who rented and sold tuxedos, but as a business owner "who made men look good."

With the pivot point of "I make men look good," he could expand his offerings to include other men's products and gift items men could give to the women in their lives. He could offer a special occasion reminder service and much more. Whatever made men look good, that is what he would offer.

In the marketing world, we talk about the importance of niching, but sometimes we niche ourselves into a box. Using a pivot point, you regain some of your freedom, flexibility, and innovation. You also expand and gain opportunities for multiple revenue streams.

In the early years of my business I didn't have much of a niche or a pivot point. If I knew how to do it and someone wanted to pay me to do it, I'd do it for them.

If someone wanted me to program a shoe store's database system or teach them how to use Microsoft Word™ or build them a web site or write an article for them, I'd do it.

In 1998 – 2000 I began working with a business/life coach. She gave me a powerful piece of advice:

"Just because you can make money at something, doesn't mean you should!"

I realized that I needed to rein in what I did and find my focus. With my business coach and Phil's help, I came up with my personal pivot point: "Highlighting truth and talent." If someone asked me to highlight truth and talent, I would consider doing it. If it didn't, I'd let that opportunity pass on by. For example, that shoe store database doesn't really highlight truth and talent. I wouldn't take on that job. Working on tedious graphic design doesn't highlight truth and talent. It might highlight a little of my talent, but if it's not fun for me why do it?

However, spotlighting authors and subject matter experts fit nicely with my pivot point of "Highlighting truth and talent."

Even today, when my business has morphed into something completely different, I still highlight truth and talent. I highlight truth in my FrontPorchSense.com blog and podcast. I share my own musical and writing talent. I encourage, support and promote my husband's talents. And, yes, I still help others share their truth and talent with the world – primarily helping them get out of their own way so their brilliance can shine through (www.MarnieKuhns.com/consulting).

That pivot point has served me for almost 15 years, and I've recently refined it further. All the while I've had the freedom and flexibility to do many different things that bring me joy as I serve others.

I've found that I'm happier and feel more sense of purpose when I operate from within my pivot point. If I stray outside it, I feel out of balance. Projects that don't fit within my pivot point hijack my time and energy, and I don't feel happy doing them. As a friend and consultant recently reminded me: "In work and in life, do what makes you happy and brings you joy."

When my husband Dave and I were dating, I was on a leadership team for a women's group that conducted a large women's event. Dave came along and assisted with the event. There were a lot of great people involved who really wanted to help others. This was something, that if we wanted to, we could continue to be a part of after the event. When we returned home, we discussed the situation, prayed about it, and realized that, for us, this opportunity was not a good fit. We couldn't get a good feeling about continuing with it. While we weren't married at the time, we knew we were heading that direction. We also didn't know exactly what we'd be doing together if we did marry. The one thing we knew was, this was not it.

Even if you aren't certain exactly what your pivot point is going to be, trust your gut throughout the process. Identifying and developing your pivot point can take time, and along the way you can still get direction about which way to turn.

The Power of an Idea

There is power behind an idea whose time has come. This story that Phil Davis shared with me is an illustration. It's about the founding of the White Squirrel Festival in Brevard, North Carolina. Many years ago, Brevard tried to have a monarch butterfly festival. Phil had just moved to town. He attended the event along with his wife and about 8 other people. The town released two monarchs at the festival. As soon as they did, one of the monarchs fell down dead.

Phil turned to his wife and said, "This doesn't seem to be the thing they should be pushing here. It seems that they would be getting behind their white squirrels." There was a White Squirrel Shop and a White Squirrel Sanctuary in the city limits. Someone brought white squirrels to Brevard in the 1950's and they had become about 25% of Brevard's squirrel population.

Phil told me, "Sometimes people don't understand that what they have is right underneath their noses."

So, Phil started asking around, "Who would I need to get with to start a White Squirrel Festival versus doing something like a Monarch Festival? Monarchs fly 10,000 miles from Canada, through North America down to Mexico. Everybody can claim some part of a Monarch, but not too many can claim a white squirrel!"

People told Phil to get with the merchant association in the heart of Brevard. Phil walked in and said, "My name is Phil Davis and I'm here to start a White Squirrel Festival." The woman he spoke to was Margaret and she said, "I don't know you. Get out of my office."

Phil said, "Well, I'll be back, Margaret."

About the third time Phil came back, Margaret said, "I know. You're Phil Davis and you want to start a White Squirrel Festival, but I don't have time for you."

The next time Phil walked in, before he could say anything, Margaret said, "Phil Davis, we're starting a White Squirrel Festival. It will be Memorial Day Weekend."

Phil asked, "Next year?"

Margaret replied, "No, in 60 days."

Phil told me, "In 60 days we had to scramble and create the first White Squirrel Festival in Brevard, North Carolina. That first year it drew about 8,000-10,000 people, which is double the entire population of the city. We were on Jay Leno. We got picked up nationwide and that event now has continued to grow and grow. It's the number one economic event in all the county. In 2011, The White Squirrel Festival drew 25,000 people to a two-day event."

"I think that's a tribute to the power of an idea that's in alignment with what's already going on in the community. All the elements were there. It's like dominos and all it needed was someone to hit that first domino. The rest of the pieces – the White Squirrel Shop, the white squirrels, the sanctuary, the things that had already been done — just began to fall like dominos and the town really rallied around it. Now folks can't imagine the town without the White Squirrel Festival," said Phil.

Your Turn

You may have everything you need all around you. What have you already started? What resources do you have? What is your white squirrel? Ask God to help you see what is right there in front of you? Ask Him to help you see your situation through His eyes. Journal what comes.

Step-By-Step Guide to Finding Your Pivot Point

Finding your pivot point doesn't have to be difficult. It will require some self-reflection and time. You also might need to try on different pivot points to see how well they serve you. Following these simple steps, you should be able to find, articulate, uncover and focus on your pivot point. Try it!

Step 1: Inventory

To find your pivot point, take an inventory of all the things you know how to do. Inventory all the different ways you've made money in the past or have served others. Rank all these things on a scale of 1 to 5, where 1 is painful for you to do and 5 is pure joy.

For example, I can list lots of things I'm good at that I've done in my life like programming websites, designing databases, answering tech questions, desktop publishing, and such. My enjoyment level from these is not what it used to be. I don't mind making my own web site or the occasional one for a friend. Doing these things day in and day out is not enjoyable for me anymore. Those would get a low score.

The things that would get my highest score have more to do with the following:

- Helping people see their greatness, their uniqueness, the wisdom and truths they can share.
- Liberating people from their limiting beliefs and past experiences that are holding their future hostage. Helping people move forward with new freedom and possibilities.
- Helping people see their next steps forward, have hope, clarity and direction and a feeling that they can do and be what they desire. They have the freedom to fly.
- Building communities of like-minded individuals who learn and grow together and experience a sense of belonging. In these communities I share the truths and wisdom I've discovered, and each member of the community can share their knowledge and wisdom and support each other
- Promoting people who have unique talents, knowledge, skills and messages that help others have hope, clarity, direction, and experience more freedom in their lives.
- Aggregating, distilling and delivering truth and freedom principles in practical, simple ways that people can understand and apply in their lives.

Step 2: Expound

Out from every item that you ranked a 4 or 5, write down what you love about it and why you love it. What does it do for you? How does it make you feel? Ask yourself, "So what?" or "I want to do this so I can do what?"

For example, I can ask myself, "Why do I love promoting people who have unique talents, knowledge, skills and messages that help others have hope, clarity, direction and experience more freedom in their lives?"

My answer: I want everyone to experience freedom. I know I can't reach everyone in the world. I don't know everything. But I do want everyone to experience freedom. So, the more people I can support and promote who are delivering liberating messages, the better. One person might have the secrets to financial freedom, another freedom from auto-immune disorders, another freedom from excess weight, another freedom from abusive relationships.

There are so many ways people can be in bondage. I want everyone to be free. And the only way for that to happen is for lots of us to be out there delivering freedom messages. When I meet someone who is liberating others, I want to shout from the rooftops about what they know and that they can help.

Step 3: Look for the Common Threads

Look for the patterns that show up in your descriptions of these joy-bringing activities. What do they all have in common? What words repeat themselves? For example, when I look at the things I love to do, I see the following themes:

- helping people
- freedom
- hope
- wisdom
- truth
- community
- clarity
- greatness

Step 4: Craft Your Pivot Point

After looking at my list, I came up with the following statement:

I'm here to distill, document and share liberating truths in simple, practical ways. I build communities where clarity, freedom and hope are fostered so participants can use their unique gifts and wisdom to liberate others.

A Bible verse that encapsulates my pivot point is Isaiah 61:1

> "The Spirit of the Lord GOD is upon me; because the LORD hath anointed me to preach good tidings unto the meek; he hath sent me to bind up the brokenhearted, to proclaim liberty to the captives, and the opening of the prison to them that are bound."

While this new pivot point is getting warmer, honestly, it's too long – too wordy. When using as few words as possible, my ultimate pivot point is Fostering Freedom.

I can use these two words "Fostering Freedom" when considering any activity or opportunity. I can ask myself, "Does this thing I'm considering foster freedom?"

It's good for me to have my longer explanation because that reminds me that sharing truth, wisdom, bringing clarity, helping people see their greatness and creating communities for people to support one another and share truths all foster freedom.

But there may be something else I haven't even thought of yet that fosters freedom. Some new thing could come along that I haven't mentioned. So, the brief pivot point of Fostering Freedom gives me a lot of breathing room and range of motion.

Step 5: Act on Your Pivot Point

As you make your list, the commonalities may jump out at you immediately. Or you may need to sit with it for a spell, sleep on it, try it on for a month or two or three. Allow it to morph if need be. You don't have to have the perfect pivot point out of the gate. Perhaps talk it out with someone you trust. Explain to them why you feel what you've chosen is your pivot point. Are you animated as you talk about it with the other person? Do you feel yourself getting jazzed about it? If so, that's a good sign. If you're already bored with it, you'll want to rethink it.

Don't worry about your pivot point being perfect. You can go forward, making a positive difference in your life and in the lives of others whether you have your pivot point perfected or not.

Your Turn

Go through these steps for your own pivot point. This is a powerful process that will bring you greater clarity and direction about who you are and why you're here on this earth. Remember clarity brings freedom and possibilities!

Pivot Points Verses Taglines

Pivot points are generally for your own internal guidance system. They are rarely something you use as a tagline. You're probably not going to put it on a business card or website. A pivot point can be a bit esoteric and cryptic.

For example, "Fostering Freedom" is probably never something I'm going to put on my website as a tagline. Freedom is a very abstract concept. It doesn't tell people enough about what benefits they are going to get from working with me.

The people I work with most likely want to know who they are and what they're here to do. They want more joy, bliss and fulfillment in their lives. They may not verbalize that as freedom.

My current tagline is "Discover, Create and Deliver Your Soul's Song."

Yes, that is probably going to change. Taglines are about what your audience needs and wants. Try on taglines and see if they're sending the message that people will resonate with. I may discover that this one isn't quite cutting it, so I'll adapt it.

Over my 30 years in business, I've used lots of taglines, but I've only had two pivot points:
- Highlighting truth and talent
- Fostering freedom

Fostering freedom gets more to the root of it – it's why I love highlighting truth and talent... it's my big why. I want more freedom for myself and others.

Fostering freedom is a refinement of highlighting truth and talent. It gives me more possibilities as it simultaneously gives me more focus. For example, someone may have an incredible talent to play basketball or cross-stitch. But neither of those are necessarily fostering freedom.

I've never felt a compulsion to sing the praises of a basketball player simply for his or her basketball talent. Yet, I will gladly tell you about my friend Donna Blevins who is 6'5" and a former basketball player who can teach you how to shift your mindset in 10 minutes or less. She has distilled a method for setting you free from your deliberating thought processes.

Multiple Income Streams

Locating Income Streams

Could you use some additional income streams? Or just a quick influx of cash flow? For many years, I was the sole provider for my family, and I know what it feels like to constantly be looking for new ways to monetize what you're doing. The following is one of those times:

I walked out into the meadow in front of my house. The green surrounded me, the sky was the clearest blue, and a gentle wind kissed my face. My husband had recently lost his job and the weight of providing for our family of eight fell squarely on my shoulders. My business was doing better than ever before, but still, I needed a few more revenue streams.

As I walked across this meadow, which had become my thinking and creation spot, I asked myself a series of questions. These questions had served me well over the years. I knew if I stepped back and looked closely at my own backyard, I would find the diamonds I needed to meet the challenge at hand.

The first questions I asked myself were...

- What problems do I see that people have that I know how to solve?
- What do I know how to do that others will gladly pay me for the knowledge?
- What are the most common questions people ask me?

The answer to the third question came easily to my mind. The question I heard most at the time was, "How do you do it all? How do you run dozens of websites, rear six children, and write so many books? How do you get so much done in so little time?"

It had never occurred to me to delve into the answer to that question. I usually brushed off the question with a laugh or a simple uninformative reply. Yet, the question was valid. How DID I get so much done? I knew a few things I did, but not enough to explain it to anyone else.

As I stood there in the meadow, I knew this was my next revenue stream – an information product that helped people get more done in a day than most people accomplish in a week.

When I got inside the house, I shot an email to a coach friend I was working with at the time. I asked her if she would be willing to interview me on the subject. She is fantastic at asking probing questions, and I knew she could draw the answers out of me.

She agreed and we set up a time for the interview. I recorded the interview and transcribed it myself. As I listen and transcribed, I added more ideas. This eventually became a profitable information product – an ebook along with some other relevant bonus items – entitled, *How to Get More Done in a Day Than Most People Accomplish in a Week.*

Since starting my business, there have been times of slow cash flow. There have also been times when what I was offering became obsolete due to changes in the marketplace. During these times, and even periodically to explore new options, I take an extensive inventory of everything I have at my disposal.

In doing so, I often find that I have acres of diamonds in my backyard. As you work toward your money goals, there are most likely resources all around you that you can use to generate the income you desire.

I'll share with you the process I go through to inventory my assets to generate quick cash and long-term revenue streams.

A Word of Advice Before Starting

You may go through this exercise and tend to think things like, "I don't own any intellectual property. I don't have a career anymore. I bring very little money into the family. I have no degrees." You may feel prone to look at this exercise the way the world looks at it ... as an assessment of net worth. You don't need careers or degrees or any money at all to make this exercise work for you.

There will be answers for which you draw a complete blank. That's okay. Some will be irrelevant for you. All we're looking for is one good idea... just one. Sometimes the idea that comes is not the ultimate idea but will move you in the direction of the answer.

Avoid looking at this exercise as an assessment of your lack. Look at it from the perspective that there is a diamond in here somewhere, and your job is to find that one diamond. The rest may be useless dirt to you at this time.

Also, the answer may not come while you perform the exercise. It may not come immediately after. It may be that this exercise harrows up the soil of your mind and an idea comes to you tomorrow, or three days from now, a week, or a month from now. Be loving with yourself and be patient with yourself. Where there is a question there is ALWAYS an answer.

Let's begin...

Gifts, Talents and Interests

First, look at your gifts, talents, and interests. Are you a great listener? Do you give excellent advice? Do you have creative skills? Perhaps you enjoy writing, teaching, speaking, creating crafts, encouraging people, rock climbing, music or yoga. Maybe you're a whiz at meditation. Maybe you are a baby whisperer. Maybe you're a great organizer, or know how to cook delicious, healthy meals. Make a big list of everything you're good at – even if you don't see how in the world it could be monetized.

Do like I did and ask yourself these three questions:

- What problems do I see that people have that I know how to solve?
- What do I know how to do that others will gladly pay me for the knowledge?
- What are the most common questions people ask me?

Resources

You most likely have at your disposal some resources that could be sold or monetized. When you inventory your resources, look at the things around your home or office that you don't use anymore. Maybe you have some rings you never wear. Maybe you have a car sitting out back that doesn't run but could be sold for the metal. Maybe you signed up for a multi-level marketing company and have an excess of product.

I'll give you an example. I once used a fat-burning bar to release 60 pounds. I finally got thin enough that I was starting to lose fat in areas that, as a woman, I wanted to keep. I stopped using the bars and had about 10 boxes at the house. While the company wouldn't let me sell their products on places like eBay, I did have a mailing list. I mailed my list and said, "Look, I used these fat burning bars to lose 60 pounds and I don't need to lose any more fat, but I have 10 boxes here. They normally sell for $14 a box, I'll let you have 10 boxes for $97. They were sold within hours.

You may have an inventory of your own products. Or maybe there are information products or virtual products you've created that you haven't sold recently. You could pull them out of your archives, give them a fresh facelift, and re-release them.

Maybe you have an excess inventory of a book you wrote that you could sell. Could you bundle the books with another product or service that you're offering? I've offered copies of 2 of my books when people purchase an hour business consult with me for the same price as a consult.

Also look at tools you own that you haven't monetized. Maybe you have a garden tiller. Could you till your neighbors' gardens for them for a fee? If you have an industrial sewing machine and yards of material, could you produce something creative with it and sell it at craft fairs? Maybe you have some video editing software and you know how to use it. Could you offer video editing services?

I have a friend whose husband suddenly became unemployed. He was handy with computers and with fixing things around the house and yard. He emailed all his neighbors and said, "I'm looking for some work. I'm handy at fixing things and can help you with household and yard work. Email me what you need fixed, I'll take the projects that are a best fit for my skills, and you pay me what it's worth to you."

He ended up putting himself and his sons to work around the neighborhood. He made the money the family needed, and before long he had an even better job than before.

What services do you currently offer, if any? Have you offered services in the past that you could offer again? Maybe you could teach a craft class or piano lessons.

If you're great with kids, you might offer babysitting or daycare services. If you're fantastic at decorations, maybe you could do party planning. If you make delicious healthy meals, maybe you could become a personal chef who prepares a week of healthy meals and brings them to people.

Start looking at your gifts, interests and talents and how they could be massaged into services you offer. Or perhaps they could be turned into information products where you teach other people how to do what you know how to do. Or maybe you could offer classes at a local community center. Perhaps you could find a rent-by-the-hour office complex and offer classes there. Some local vocational schools hire people to teach classes. Check in your area for opportunities.

People

Lastly, but certainly not least, inventory the people in your life – especially the people you know who have connections or who have special skills, talents, products or services. How could you joint venture with these people?

It may be that your own teenager has special skills. I was at a mastermind recently and the woman running the mastermind had a 17-year-old daughter who was great at photography. While the mastermind was going on, her daughter did headshots for anyone who wanted one for $36.

This expanded the value of the woman's mastermind and gave her daughter a way to generate her own income. When you help your children create their own income that saves you money! Saved money is found money!

If you're an essential oils rep, you might buddy up with someone who is good at marketing. He or she could come train your team. This would enhance the success of your team and perhaps if someone on your team wanted to purchase the marketing consultant's products or services you could make an affiliate commission on the sale.

How could you enrich what you do for your existing clients and customers by creating joint-products and services with others? How can you earn affiliate commissions by introducing people to what other people are offering? If you're the kind of person who makes recommendations and people follow your recommendations, you don't have to have any product, service or skill of your own. You could just make money off referrals.

As you gather your inventory, open your mind to the possibilities. It may be that you come up with an idea that will work well for you in the next 3 months. It may not be something you want to do long term, but it's a quick cash crop for you. Other ideas may be more long-term producers.

As you create revenue streams think of them as a garden. You have your summer produce like beans, squash, and cucumbers. They grow for a few months and you can preserve them for later. But they aren't going to keep growing long term. Then there are fruit trees that may not generate anything edible for years, but when they do start producing, they'll feed you for a lifetime.

As you review your inventory, look for the short-term producers and the long-harvest crops. Have a healthy mix of both.

Your Turn

Take out a piece of paper and go through these areas and inventory what you have at your disposal. Then get creative on finding the acres of diamonds in your own backyard.

Act

Once you've performed this exercise and given yourself time to formulate some possible ideas, remember what I did in the story at the beginning. ACT. I went inside the house and emailed my coach friend. That was not a huge action. I didn't immediately write the ebook. But I did take one step toward being able to do so.

Take one action... the obvious first action. The first action might be simply deciding which of your ideas to start first. Which one of your better ideas would be the easiest for you to complete in the fastest amount of time? I usually start there because action leads to action.

The success of completing one idea will give you the momentum to move into another. More success is held hostage by indecision than anything else. Don't get hung up on which idea.

Some people obsess for so long over which idea to pursue they could have implemented three in their indecision time. Pick one with potential that you can implement the fastest. Then DO IT.

Remember If you will act fast upon inspiration, you will be led to the next action, and the next and the next. Before long, you will have accomplished your objective.

Stabilizing Your Cash Flow

If you've done your homework and have a good idea of your pivot point, you want to think bigger than creating quick cash flow. You want to create systems for smoothing out your cash flow long term. If you know what your pivot point is, it's time to create multiple income streams within it. For example, when I operated IdeaMarketers as a content directory, some of my multiple income streams included the following:

- Book Sales
- Newsletter builder subscription service
- Expert Program – PR/Marketing subscription
- Set-Your-Own-Price Bidding System – where people decided how much they wanted to pay to have their article on the home page of IdeaMarketers. They could pay as little as $1/week. Articles were sorted from highest to lowest bidder. Some people paid up to $100 or more for a week of top positioning.
- Pay-Per-Click Ad Revenue was one of our biggest revenue streams. We were paid a small amount every time a visitor clicked

on an ad. With over 10 million pageviews served each month, this translated into a six-figure income annually most years.
* Consulting by the hour
* Speaking

There was a combination of low-priced monthly services, higher-priced monthly services, and the options for one-time purchases or repeat purchases. Also notice the passive revenue from advertising and even some hourly rate services. While consulting by the hour was one of the revenue streams, it wasn't a primary one. Most of the revenues were quite passive.

There were some summers I took off work completely and let the site run via automation and delegation. When you get away from trading hours-for-dollars, you open yourself up to greater freedom and more revenues.

Think of your business as a garden. Your revenue streams are crops. Ideally, you'll have a combination that gives you year-round cash flow. If what you do is seasonal, find ways to flesh out your off seasons. For example, in this business, pay-per-click ad revenue was always sluggish in the summers. So was consulting. Monthly subscriptions smoothed out our cash flow.

Ideally, you'll have some fruit trees and nut trees in your garden that produce every year. Fruit trees don't produce for the first 3-5 years, but once they get going, you can usually count on them year after year. In the beginning of IdeaMarketers, the site was a lot like a young fruit tree. It didn't have enough traffic to make advertising revenues an option. Eventually, the site became so well-known and there was so much traffic that I could have done nothing but run ads and been fine.

I can almost hear the question coming from your lips. You're probably wondering why I'm talking about this web site in the past. It still exists, but not in the form it once did.

The answer is a perfect illustration for why it's important to have multiple income streams. When one or more of them dry up, you aren't devastated.

In my situation with IdeaMarketers, Google pulled our pay-per-click ads which cut out a little over 1/3 of the revenues. I had other revenue streams that would have kept the site going nicely. But Google wasn't satisfied in pulling the ads. They also began punishing anyone who put content into IdeaMarketers. If there were links going to a person's web site from IdeaMarketers, Google delisted the person's site. Their site got dropped out of Google search results completely. This meant our Expert program, our bidding system and basically the whole site was toast.

I couldn't, in integrity, tell people to keep putting their content into my site and let Google punish them.

I won't digress into all the monopolistic reasons I believe Google did this. Suffice it to say, I shut the site down in early 2013, and focused on my remaining revenue streams:

- Consulting
- Speaking / Teaching
- Book Publishing and Sales
- Helping other people get their books in print.

Even though my biggest revenue streams were gone, I still had some revenue streams. I also had the relationships I'd forged over the years. These relationships enabled me to leverage what I was doing to joint venture partners' audiences. (I'll discuss more about that type of joint venturing and collaboration later.)

While my story is a cautionary tale, it's also one that illustrates the power of multiple revenue streams. The more you have, the better off you'll be if something destroys your orchard.

Accentuate the Positive

I'll talk more about gratitude in a later chapter, but I'd like to address the importance of looking for the good in our lives. Over the years I've had seasons in my business when I worked long work hours, volunteered in my church, reared six kids, all while trying to be a good wife. My mother always expressed concern if she felt I was taking on too much. She worried for me and did everything she could to lighten my load.

Sometimes, I was tempted to have a bit of a pity party with my mom by phone because she was a wonderful shoulder to lean on. Throughout everything I have done in my life, my mother was my cheerleader, my confidant, my greatest fan. I believe there is nothing more priceless in life than to have someone who believes in you, who will acknowledge the heavy burdens you carry, show sympathy, but also have the faith that somehow, someway you're going to pull through.

There came a point in my business where I began to realize that complaining or having those pity parties were not helping me. I learned that my business was a lot like a baby. Babies are barometers of their mothers. If a mother is stressed out and upset, her baby's going to start squalling. If the mother is calm and serene, her baby usually is too.

The calmer and more positive I was about my life and my business, the more smoothly it ran. My dad used to say, "Money comes easily except when you really need it badly." The needier you are, the more you repel what you're wanting. If you have a calm, relaxed, expectant attitude, things come to you more naturally.

Eventually, I told my mom, "I can't afford to be negative. It affects my bottom line." So we stopped having those pity parties. She still encouraged me and still was aware of what I dealt with, but we kept things on more of a positive note. Did it help? Yes! Especially now, I can see that this attitude shift made a difference.

Sometimes no matter how much you know you should be more positive; you can't seem to get yourself in a positive space.

As I mentioned earlier, in late 2012, Google made changes that destroyed IdeaMarketers' viability as a content directory. Rather than continue operating the site, I decided to shut it down and focus on my Light the World movement and help people get books into print. This cut my revenues to a sixth of what they had been.

What's more, while I still had my contacts and relationships I'd built, I did not have the ability to put things into my site and get them noticed the way I once could.

I hung on for a few years, doing the best I could, but eventually, it all caught up with me financially.

In March of 2017 my second husband unexpectedly told me he wanted a divorce and my mother (who had been very ill) died four days later. After going to her funeral, I was basically homeless (living with my dad). I felt I was at the lowest of the low. Even my computer crashed the day my mom died, and my only car went on the fritz shortly after. I felt like I was living the old country song, "If it weren't for bad luck, I'd have no luck at all. Gloom, despair and agony on me ... Woah!"

During this time, someone told me about a book called, *The Breakthrough Experience* by Dr. John Demartini. Because I was desperate for answers, I read the book and did the exercise in it. To my surprise (but not to my friend's), I had an incredible breakthrough that completely changed the way I view life.

I learned that we do not have to be positive all the time. It's not necessary. We just need to see things realistically. When we put something or someone on a pedestal, we aren't looking at them realistically. Equally true is that when we put something or someone in a pit, we're not seeing realistically, either. The truth is this: Everything has two sides within it.

Every situation has challenges and support within it. Every person has lights and shadows. As human beings, we need support and we need challenges. Divine love, which fills the universe, sees to it that we have both.

So, if there's something in your life that is a little bit bad, there's a little bit of good in it too. If it's catastrophic, there is something phenomenal in it. Not down the road, but right now — in the present. Yes, there's good coming down the road too, but it's also good right here and now.

The thing is you must have eyes to see it. As I began applying the principles I learned in *The Breakthrough Experience*, I realized that nothing is ever lost. It just changes form. My mother wasn't lost. She was just in the next room. I felt her near. I heard her speaking to me in my mind. I felt her love magnified and amplified in ways that were truly miraculous. She showed up in random words spoken by strangers or in friends' or children's' actions.

I also learned about the concept of divine compensation or compensating blessings. Within everything bad is something good. There is a divine balance, an opposition in all things. Whenever you encounter a challenge, start looking around for the treasure (the compensating blessings). It's like the video games my kids like to play. In these games, you don't just randomly receive rewards. You must jump hurdles, perform feats, defeat enemies. And whenever you overcome a challenge, you can look around for the prize – the coin, the points, the extra lives. It's that way for us. By divine law, we are always compensated.

Eventually, I recovered from my multiple traumas – faster than anyone could imagine — due to the things I learned in that book. I met someone who in so many ways is much like my mother. His listening ear, generosity and the way he believes in me and unconditionally loves me, the way he is my biggest fan, is so much like my mother that it's uncanny. He is my divine compensation. Eventually, all the "things" I lost were restored.

My life changed after this. I began to look at my life with the understanding that everything I need is with me, right here in this moment. I just need to be observant and look around to see where it is. If I'm not seeing it, I'm not looking hard enough.

Seeing the Truth as It Really Is

One of the hardest things for me was letting go of past successes and allowing myself to move in a new direction. When IdeaMarketers "died," a part of me died too.

For several years on some level I grieved the loss of the successful business woman I once was. I didn't walk around in grief. I wasn't depressed, negative or angry. But the fact that I "used to have" something incredibly successful and innovative and that I once pioneered the entire article marketing industry was hard to live up to. Nothing I did or created for the next several years seemed "good enough" in comparison. The specter of my own success relentlessly loomed in the catacombs of my subconscious.

I grieved the loss of that success and that business and that prominence. Still, as I moved forward with my life and my career objectives, I realized this vital truth: I had no desire to do the type of work I once did. Tech work is not who

I am. There were downsides to owning a large content directory. While it gave me a lot of freedom to voluntarily help people build their businesses and to speak, teach, inspire, and write, there were also stretches of intense 60-70+ hour work weeks. There were times when I lost who I was and what I was about and even what I thought about, simply because work was so all-consuming.

Remembering the Challenges

We tend to remember past successes as all rosy and wonderful, but every situation has its challenges. Part of getting over the past is seeing it realistically for what it was.

Part of the reason I wrote this book is that I finally put away my rose-colored glasses that I was viewing my successful past through. I remembered the entire, realist truth. Was I successful? Yes! But there were downsides. Big ones! For example:

Russians and Chinese hackers loved to have a field day with my site and often injected garbage code in my database of 3+ million articles. Cleaning up the mess, programming patches to keep hacks from happening again, and removing garbage articles input by bots often became a living nightmare.

People put nasty materials into my site which I had to create filters for. Here I was, trying to help what I call "Light Bearers" get their positive messages into the world, and much of my time was spent looking at and creating filters to remove nasty, dark material from my website. And many people have said, any time you deal with filth — even if you're doing it in a good way and with good intentions — you're going to get some of it on you.

For a while, I missed the influence I once had. I missed the impact I could make. I missed being able to get positive messages into the world in an economical way. And yet, I had no desire to go back to the tedium of tech work. Then I had the opportunity to attend a live event. While there, people kept coming up to me and saying they enjoyed following me on social media, reading my blog posts, and getting my emails. What I had to say meant something to them. One woman came in tears, thanking me for sharing my difficult experiences because reading what I shared helped her process her own pain.

I mentioned this to my husband when I returned from the event and he said, "Everything people mentioned wasn't from your IdeaMarketers days. It was who you are NOW and what you're sharing NOW. You are making an impact NOW. Let go of 'I used to...'"

I had been living my life remembering the past as the glory days... the days when I could make an impact by sheer numbers. What I discovered is that quantity isn't necessarily quality. Just because IdeaMarketers served up 10 million pageviews a month during the height of its success, didn't mean those 10 million pages were impacting lives, really touching and transforming hearts. More isn't necessarily better. It's just more.

What touches hearts is vulnerability, honesty, and really caring. That is what my hardships gave me – vulnerability. They made me real, raw and relevant, and people can connect with that.

Today, I have lots of free time to explore my interests, expand my talents, and learn new things that interest me. I'm able to be a voice for things I believe in and not worry about whether people agree with me or not. I don't filter what I say based on whether I might lose business over a stand I make on something I feel is important.

I used to wear the word "Busy" like a badge of honor.

"How have you been?" a friend would ask.

"Busy," came my reply.

That word meant I was productive, valuable, significant.

Not anymore.

I've finally created a peaceful, serene, simple life where I focus on reflection, observation, developing talents, self-expression, service, and creating what brings me joy and fulfillment. It's a wonderful place to be. It's liberating to be in a place where I'm not running from one project or place to another. Rather, I start each day asking God what He'd like me to do, and many times He answers, "Whatever brings you joy."

Shifting the Way I See the World

When I first learned the principles taught in *The Breakthrough Experience*, I saw everything with radically realistic vision. I saw the upsides and the downsides of every situation. Seeing both sides neutralized some of the infatuation or the joy to be found in new positive things. But it also took the sting out of things that seemed "bad."

At first, I wondered, "Is this how I must live my life now – in this flat, almost unemotional state where nothing is fantastic, and nothing is horrible? It's all just a combination of both?"

In a way, the answer to that is yes. But in another way, it's not. Things still happen that challenge me. People still do things that get on my nerves. I've gone through some painful events and experiences. But now I see the other side that goes with that pain. For example, when someone drops out of my life because they decide they don't like me, I'm learning (because of my new perspective) that they probably just made room for someone new and better suited to come into my life.

I've started to see the challenges in my life as blessings. The pain and the challenge and the difficulties are the "price" I pay to have the upside to the downside. I focus on the good things. With great gratitude, I say, "Okay, I really love this and it's worth the price of the challenge laced within it." If the good doesn't appear to equal the bad, then I need to look for more good things. They're there. I just need to open my eyes to see them.

It's been a fun game to start looking for the compensating blessings to be found in any challenging situation. It's always there. It may take some prayer and patience, but I always find it.

I've even started going a step further and expressing gratitude for the challenges because they make the good things possible. I have some people in my life who have been unkind. Now whenever I'm tempted to be irritated about how they've treated me, I go to gratitude. I thank them in my mind for being the counterweight to my wonderful, amazing life. They make the good possible – by being the counterbalance. I thank them for playing that role, and then I feel peace about things as they really are. I'm able to rejoice in the good more.

Are You An Inspired Creative?

You've heard my story. Now, let's talk about you! Do you have tons of ideas for projects, products, and services that could make the world a better place? Do you get a thrill out of those "aha moments" of life and have an intense desire to share what you discover with others?

Have you ever felt disgusted with yourself when you didn't run with a big idea fast enough and a few months later saw someone else turn the same idea into a screaming success? Have you experienced the exhilaration of a new idea only to have your zest for it wane as it came time to implement all the details to make it happen?

If this describes you, you very well could be an Inspired Creative. Imagine with me for a moment that heaven is raining down ideas — all kinds of technological, scientific, self-growth, medical, artistic, and spiritual truth. It's all being broadcast across the earth, trusting that someone who resonates with each idea will act upon it and follow through.

Everyone has the capability of tapping into this broadcast system. Some people are more receptive to the broadcast than others. Some are more likely to act than their neighbors.

There is a small percentage of the population who are almost hardwired to this "channel of ideas." These people love to inspire others with the insights that come to them through their hardwired connection to inspiration.

Inspired Creatives have so many ideas, they find it almost impossible to pick just one or two to work on. If you ask an Inspired Creative to select his favorite movie, for example, he'd have a hard time doing so. He might find it equally difficult to select only one "best friend." He would never want to narrow the possibilities to just one of anything.

Inspired Creatives are hooked up to heaven's channel of inspiration like a fire hose. They get so many ideas it would be impossible for one person to implement them all.

While having a hard wire to inspiration sounds like a wonderful advantage (and it is), there are downsides for the Inspired Creatives of the world.

Have You Fallen into the "All or Nothing Trap?"

The typical Inspired Creative assumes the immense flow of ideas she has are all for her. She may think every idea that comes along should be followed through upon. How overwhelming is that? How in the world would she know where to start? And when you encourage the Inspired Creative to "just pick one of those ideas," she feels paralyzed. Why? She knows that, in choosing one, it means thousands of other equally brilliant ideas with fantastic potential are rejected.

This makes it difficult for entrepreneurial Inspired Creatives to select a niche. Because they can't select just one, they have difficulty marketing themselves. They flit from one idea to the next, never laying hold on anything long enough to create a good product funnel or effectively market their expertise.

I have an Inspired Creative friend who decided to narrow her niche down specifically to one group of people who wanted one service. Within a week, she felt horrible, stooped over, unable to get out of bed and plagued with an unexplainable depression. After talking with her on the phone for about fifteen minutes, we dug down to the root of the situation. We discovered that she was grieving all the lost possibilities. It was as if they had literally died and she'd attended their funeral. We worked to clear the grief and within a few more minutes, she was walking straight with a spring in her step and a smile on her face. The burden was lifted and she was able to focus on serving her niche, which in turn brought her incredible joy.

Are You a Victim of "The Squirrel Syndrome?"

Did you ever see Disney's movie Up? In it, the dogs can talk, and they are easily distracted. Mid-sentence their heads dart to the side as they bark, "Squirrel!" Inspired Creatives often suffer from chronic Squirrel Syndrome.

Why is this? Ideas take time to implement. So, let's say an Inspired Creative starts an idea. That doesn't mean the storm of ideas has stopped coming for her.

That's why an Inspired Creative with a project is easily distracted onto something else mid-stream before ever taking her initial idea to completion. Sometimes Inspired Creatives assume they are ADD, when really, it's not a physical or chemical malady, but a lack of understanding of how their minds work.

Do Those Big Ideas Eventually Become Boring to You?

The typical Inspired Creative has a tough time following an idea through to completion because she can become bored with it before it's implemented. This happens for two reasons. First, the Inspired Creative thrives on inspiration. There's a "high" associated with a new idea, and she's like an "inspiration junkie." While the idea is new and fresh, her passion fuels her energy and propels her forward. But once the idea has become old and "stale" she's looking for the next big idea... her next "high."

Another reason the Inspired Creative becomes bored is that there is a cycle to creativity. One of the phases in it is a Rest phase. To an Inspired Creative, that Rest phase feels like:

- Apathy
- Boredom
- A diminished connection to inspiration

Inspiration doesn't completely cease for these individuals, but it can feel like it's slowed to a trickle. For the Inspired Creative (who is used to a fire-hose flow) it may as well have ceased. The withdrawals are intense and can even look like depression!

If an Inspired Creative doesn't successfully launch and implement an idea before reaching the Rest phase, she may abandon the idea completely.

Therefore, it is important to understand which phase of the creative process you are in and why it's so important to gain clarity about your focus. I'll explain what those phases are shortly.

You Can Stay Focused, Complete Your Big Ideas, and Generate Income!

When an Inspired Creative learns the natural ebbs and flows of her creative cycle, she can work with nature, instead of against it. Imagine the increased passion and energy you'll enjoy when you know you're living your life's purpose! Imagine what it would be like to take your big ideas to the finish line and reap the rewards from them! Imagine what it would be like to know what ideas to pursue and which ones are taking you off task like "Squirrel!"

If you're an Inspired Creative who would like to work with passion and purpose in a focused direction that fulfills your creativity and meets your craving desire to impact the world in a positive way, then please read the next few chapters. Even if you don't feel you're an Inspired Creative, you still have a creative cycle. The next few chapters will help you understand and be more powerful in your creative cycle.

I'll be giving you an overview of the creative process so you can easily decide where you are and what you should be doing in each phase to navigate it smoothly. As you do this, you'll be able to follow your bliss and get more done. As you do so, money will flow.

THE PHASES OF THE CREATIVE PROCESS

The State of Flow

For an Inspired Creative, a state of Flow is when ideas and inspiration come to you effortlessly as if you're tuning into a channel. It's as if there's a hardwired connection into your brain like a cord, feeding ideas and inspiration, epiphanies and analogies. When you're in a state of Flow, things that you do come easier for you. If we were to compare it to nature, it would be the season of spring when flowers are blooming, and new foliage is popping up.

Sports athletes hit a state of Flow where they can't miss. I remember one basketball game in high school where I made 16 free throws in a game. I was "in the zone" or in a state of Flow that night.

You can hardly mess up when you're in this state. Flow is a wonderful place to be. It's a natural high. When we're not in Flow, we're longing for it and wanting to go back to it. It's sort of like the movie Star Trek Generations where Malcom McDowell's character (Soran) and his ship of people enter the Nexus, a nirvana-like state where anything is possible. Mistakenly, the U.S.S. Enterprise crew believes that Soran and his people are in danger and attempt to save them by beaming them aboard the Enterprise. Soran and his people are jerked from the Nexus; and they are devastated that they have been removed from this place of bliss. Soran is so desperate, he begins a quest to do anything and everything to get back to the Nexus — including destroying stars and entire solar systems to reroute the Nexus into his path.

That's the way Flow is for many of us. It's wonderful, exhilarating. Anything is possible. And when we've lost it, we long for it with a homesickness that makes us desperate. Like the Nexus, Flow isn't something you can manipulate or coerce. You put yourself in its path and it comes in its own time and in its own way. Unlike Soran, we can't destroy stars to change the gravitational path of our Flow state. We must wait for it to come naturally.

It's important to document what's coming to you when you're in a state of Flow. You're going to hit phases of the creative process where you won't be able to find the Flow state. In those phases, you can lean on your past Flow states to guide you — IF you've documented them and kept your focus. Make a practice of keeping a journal, log or notebook of your ideas.

There have been times when I've gotten very clear visuals of what is possible for me. After these revelations came, things fell apart completely. And even though it looked like there was no way my big dream would ever be a reality, in time, it miraculously happened. When the time was right, my big dream happened faster and more incredibly than anyone would believe.

What got me through the tough times were journal entries that I wrote in the original Flow state. I documented those visions. Now as I sit down with my husband and share those journal entries, we marvel at the miraculous way everything unfolded. As we read the entries, you'd think they were written in the present, now, from our life today, and not from seven, eight or nine years ago, before we even knew each other.

Another thing I recommend is having a master list. One of my coaches taught me this around 2000. A master list is not a "to do list." It's a place to hold all your ideas. Some you may implement, some you may give away, and others you may save for another time. You can pull ideas from this master list throughout the phases of the creative process.

If you've written all your ideas down on separate pieces of paper, take a little time to consolidate all your ideas in one place on your master list. I use an Excel spreadsheet for this. You can get a copy of mine at www.MarnieKuhns.com/creatives

Production

The second phase of the creative process is Production. The energy and excitement you felt in your state of Flow doesn't immediately disappear. It leads into an action state where you start creating things. If we were to compare this phase in nature, it would be summer, when gardens produce fruits and vegetables.

The Flow state usually takes you into a state of action, taking steps toward your idea. When you find an idea that excites you and really resonates with you, it propels you into action. You start working on the idea and doing what you know to do — assuming you don't have any emotional, mental or energetic blocks stopping you from acting.

If you see that you have trouble acting on ideas, then there may be some blocks there that you'll want to take care of. But let's assume you have that natural momentum from the idea that takes you into action. Eventually you'll get into a zone where it's not taking a lot of creativity or new ideas. It's more the act of doing and taking consistent action.

As you move from the Flow state into Production, sometimes you'll start to do redundant tasks that do not take a lot of mental effort. You'll get a lot done, but you're not necessarily doing something new or exciting. The outcomes may be new, but the skills, tasks and resources are things you know how to use. You're implementing them onto the new idea.

I call the Production phase my workaholic zone. In the old days, I could work up to 14 hours a day in the Production zone because I had a burst of energy that propelled me toward completing the idea. Generally, while you're in this, you can be oblivious to what's going on in the world around you. You're sort of like a workhorse with blinders on. Your family and other relationships often take a backseat when you're in this phase of the creative process.

A friend once told me about a book she read about Leonardo DiVinci. He would go into his workshop and be engrossed for days on end. People wouldn't see him because he was in the zone working on his project. Then he would leave the workshop and disappear. That is because he moved out of the productive phase and moved into the third phase of the creative process.

Organization

While you're engrossed in what you're doing in the Production phase, your energy eventually starts to wane. You suddenly come to your senses and realize your house is a mess, your kids have been eating Raman noodles for two weeks, your desk is chaotic, and your laundry is stacked in piles. If you're a mom, you're going to feel guilty at this point. You'll most likely start beating yourself up that your kids have been living on cheap pasta and toaster pastries. You can get yourself into a depressed state over the guilt.

Another thing that might happen is that you'll realize that you need to do something about the mess. You'll go into organizational mode. You'll clean the house, catch up on the laundry, organize your desk, organize your office. Maybe you'll make a meal chart or a chore chart for your family. You'll try to take control and rein in your environment that went to pot while you were in the Production phase.

The Organization phase is equivalent to autumn in nature. It's when you harvest your produce, bottle it, dehydrate it, freeze it and store it away for the winter.

The Organization phase does not have to be chaotic. Yes, you do have cycles that you go through. But you can put systems in place that run your household, business and office while you're in the Flow and Production phases so you don't emerge from them to discover your world in chaos.

Systems to Reduce Stress and Keep Your Life Flowing

The first system you should put in place is delegation. Delegate wherever you can. Start with your family. If there is someone in your home who likes doing consistent tasks like cooking, shopping, or running errands, assign them to do those tasks.

This way your household can run more smoothly. When I was working long hours with six kids at home, I used to hire a woman to come on Fridays and do a deep clean on my house. This way it never got too far out of whack.

As far as my business, there were newsletters that needed to go out. There were audios and videos and inspiration of the day that need to be broadcast consistently. There was client promotion that had to be done. There's no way that I, as an Inspired Creative, was going to be able to keep up with those day-to-day tasks. So,

I hired a savvy friend to be my right-hand-assistant. For a decade, my friend worked alongside me, brainstorming new ideas, helping me implement them, managing client accounts and keeping my business running smoothly. My business never took off in a big way until I hired her. It was one of the best things I ever did to grow my business.

Currently my husband and I work the business together and divide tasks based on our strengths and interests. We hire one of my daughters to create social media graphics for author clients. While I enjoy creating graphics, I only enjoy it in spurts. It needs to be done consistently, and she enjoys doing something creative on the side of her day job.

Over the years, I've learned to be more consistent in some ways, but the best way I know to bring consistency to a business is to automate or delegate. I know my nature. I get bored doing the day-to-day minutiae. Rather than force myself to do something that drains my energy and creativity, I delegate or automate. For example, I have integrated my email system with my web site so that when I post a new blog, an email with the latest posts periodically goes out through an email via automation.

The trick is to set up systems. Look at all the things you do and create systems so that things don't fall apart when you're in Flow and Production. Look at the needs of your home, family, business, and health. Delegate where you can and create habits and systems.

There are some things you can't delegate – like exercising regularly and eating healthfully. Create a ritual for those things. Have set times and days that you work out. Make a habit of buying healthy foods. Consider making things ahead of time and refrigerating or freezing them so that meal prep is easy when you're busy.

I have a checklist you can use for daily tasks. I use a chart that reminds me to perform daily tasks that can't be delegated. These include my personal spiritual practice, exercising, taking vitamins, and practicing the piano. In my busy times I've kept this chart on my office wall by my computer monitor so I can see it daily.

You can download this Excel spreadsheet at www.MarnieKuhns.com/creatives

Rest Phase

I used to call this phase "boredom" or "apathy." In nature, the Rest phase is winter. Nothing grows. Everything seems to die. For an Inspired Creative, it can be a mind-numbing state that can even feel like depression. As Inspired Creatives, we fight rest. We want the energy and exhilaration of Flow and Production. Rest feels like someone unplugged our hardwire to inspiration. We're like a junky who can't get our drug of choice. We feel abandoned, disconnected and often apathetic toward our projects. We don't care about them anymore. We may even decide they are boring.

My father used to come up with grand ideas. For example, one time he decided he would build a golf course. He went to work on his bulldozer in the Production phase. He moved dirt. He dug ponds, and he made sand traps. Then the natural burnout that comes after you've worked yourself that hard came. He lost all interest in the golf course. He laid on the couch for a few weeks. He worked minimally at his day job as a dentist and then came home and rested on the couch. He said he was thinking, but my mom thought he was the laziest man on the planet.

When he came back around to his next flow state, the golf course was no longer of interest to him. Instead he went off on a new project, like building a trailer park.

The more prolonged the Rest phase (where you're bored and apathetic about your idea) the more likely it is that when you hit a state of Flow, you'll be off on a new idea. This is why my mother drummed into our heads, "Finish what you start. Finish what you start." Hers is the voice inside my head.

Well-known marketing mentor Adam Urbanski once told me that he selects projects he can finish in 72 hours. He didn't say why, but I believe it's because he's an Inspired Creative. He knows that if he doesn't finish it in that amount of time, he's going to lose interest and won't get it done. Know yourself and know that you're probably not going to finish something if it takes too much time.

I highly recommend that Inspired Creatives track their moods. Track the phase you think you're in. Ask yourself, "Was I full of new ideas and epiphanies today?" If so, you were in a state of Flow. "Did I get a lot done today that didn't require new thinking?" If so, it's Production. For example, programming for me is a Production activity. I may be creating something new, but I'm using knowledge that I already have in order to accomplish it. I'm past the idea phase and now I'm implementing.

Track your phases for as long as you can. If you'll do it for a month, you'll start to see patterns. You'll start to see how long you can stay in the Flow and Production states before you need a Rest phase. Your Rest seems to be proportional to the amount of energy you expended in the other three phases (Flow, Production and Organization).

For example, in June and July of 2011, I was in major Production mode. I taught technical knowledge at an event. Then I went into redesigning IdeaMarketers. My daughter created the design, but I had to apply it to thousands of pages of code to implement it. Again, this was nothing new or creative. It was Production. Once we'd done that, we noticed that people were miscategorizing articles. There were gardening articles in the business category and parenting articles in the automotive category.

I set my kids in front of computers and we started recategorizing these articles. This was a tedious Organization phase. I worked many 12-14 hour days in this Organizational phase. I spent nearly two months doing work that is not my natural passion. Quite the opposite.

Because I was doing work that is not my natural personality, I crashed. By the time August came around, I couldn't think of a new idea. When a friend called wanting me to brainstorm with her, I had to send her away. I couldn't even go there. At the end of August, my family went on a vacation to the beach for a month. Normally in a nature setting, my analogies and creative epiphanies starts to flow. Nothing. They didn't happen. We played lots of Go Fish. We sat on the beach and made sandcastles and my brain did not function at a business level at all. I didn't force myself to go there.

The day after I got back, I kicked back into a Flow state. You have to have enough rest to compensate for the energy you spent in your Production phase. Inspired Creatives are drained by staying in tedium for too long.

So, track your cycles. You'll see little cycles and big cycles. I have cycles within cycles. Many years I hit a Rest phase in the summer. For you it may be winter, fall or spring. You will have a macro cycle and a micro cycle. Be aware of yourself. Schedule yourself accordingly.

Get familiar with how your body works. Some people feel they have a cycle within the day. They might have less energy first thing in the morning. Then they hit their stride. They may want to take a nap in the afternoon and then get a second wind in the evening.

Listen to your body. Relax into the Rest. Go ahead and take the vacation. Don't strain yourself. I know that's hard. Even when I know I'm supposed to be resting, there is the guilt that crops up.

"I'm not accomplishing anything. I have work to do. I should be able to be creative." At a visceral level, we struggle with the Rest phase and feel it is somehow wrong. Despite that, know that the Rest is necessary, and it will serve you in the long run. It's all part of the cycle.

I worked with a client once who had reached such a level of burnout in her business that she decided to step back from it and take a bit of a sabbatical. She did the bare minimum and took several months to focus on her family, explore her creativity and enjoy life.

After a while, she began to panic, feeling like she might never find her creative flow again. It came only in sputters but nothing solid. By the time she called me, she'd lost her focus and her direction. She could barely drag herself out of bed in the mornings and was riddled with guilt as a result.

We talked through where she was in the creative cycle, and I pointed out that she was in the Rest phase and that she should just relax into it and allow herself to explore what gave her joy in life. We cleared a few mental blocks and the guilt she felt about taking this rest. We reframed the Rest phase into a good thing — a quest to explore what brought her true joy. As we hung up the phone, I encouraged her, "You can do this! You can do nothing!"

A couple days later, I shot her an email and asked her how "doing nothing" was going for her. She said she was on a creative roll. Things were falling into place. She had a clear direction and was in "the zone." All she needed was to give herself permission to rest. By the next day she'd moved back into another flow.

This is the power of surrender!

The quicker you allow the Rest, the better. My father lying on the couch was probably the best thing that he could do. What we'll talk about next is once you have taken the Rest, how to come back to task and not get sidetracked onto a new idea that takes you off task.

Staying Focused

The place we are most vulnerable to distraction is right after the Rest phase when we hit a new Flow state (when spring rolls around again). It's like someone hooks us back to the inspirational channel. All these new ideas are flowing again, and it's very tempting to get sidetracked on bright and shiny new ideas. The best antidote for distraction is focus.

I used to have an arrowhead necklace that I got from a Navajo woman in Old Town Albuquerque, New Mexico. It reminded me to follow my heart and stay focused. Create your own talisman that reminds you to stay focused. If you know who you are and what you're here to do, it's much easier to stay focused.

For example, in the early days of my business, if someone asked me to program a site that sells toys, I would have done it. Today I would not. It's outside my focus. My purpose is to foster freedom. So, if a new idea comes along, yes it could make me money. But if it's outside my focus, I don't do it. Remember your pivot point! Remember: "Just because you can make money at something, doesn't mean you should!"

Remember that when new opportunities come your way (for example, the hot new MLM program your neighbor brings over), you don't have to do that. Yes, it may be a cool idea and even be interesting. But is it a natural fit? For example, I know selling a product (even if it's based on a true principle) is off tangent for me. I know that when I'm marketing, I love promoting people. I lose interest in things, but I never lose interest in people. The more you refine who you are, who you serve, and what you're here to do, the better off you'll be. Once you've narrowed down your pivot point, you can see if things fit.

The ideas you get may not be for you. Remember that when you're hardwired into a channel of inspiration, you could be getting ideas that are meant to be given to someone else. You might be getting an idea you could give your neighbor or your client. Share the wealth of ideas that are coming to you. Believe it or not, there are some people who are never hardwired to inspiration or creative ideas. They never know what that feels like. You've got tons of ideas. You don't need them all! Some of them could belong to the people around you. They're worth gold to them. You're the receptor.

Keep your master list of ideas and start breaking it down between the things that are around your pivot point and those that aren't. You can keep the ones that aren't, and they may be something you share with someone else who needs a good idea. You could categorize them if you get tons of ideas. If you're all over the board with your ideas, write them down, but stick with and implement the ones that fit your focus.

What to Do When You're Stuck

An important lesson I learned when I was doing a lot of programming was what to do when you get stuck. Sometimes you can be working on something and no matter what you do, it just doesn't work. This happened a lot when I was programming databases. I'd be in my office for hours trying to figure out some little thing and my husband would tell me, "Take a break." I would roll my eyes at him and grumble something about how I didn't have time to take a break, I had to figure this out.

He'd insist again that I needed to take a break. Eventually, I'd do it. I'd go do something like washing dishes and then come back and there, right in front of my face I'd notice a missing semicolon or some other miniscule thing that was throwing off my programming. It would be so obvious when I returned from my break.

Over the years, I've tried to remember this. If I'm stuck – take a break. Don't keep stewing in your juices or overanalyzing things. Step back, do something different and then when you return the solution will often be obvious.

Your Turn

Where are you feeling stuck? Is there a specific project that isn't clicking for you? Is there an area of your business that is struggling? Is there a relationship that isn't working for you? How can you step back and do something else for a while and return with fresh eyes? Is there something else you'd like to work on right now instead? If you're experiencing a significant challenge, maybe you could take a day off and do something fun? Or go away for the weekend. At the very least, go for a walk in nature! Clear your head.

One of the best ways for me to gain perspective on my life is to travel. There's something about being in a plane and going somewhere completely different that shifts my perspective on life. What can you do — even in some small way to step away from the thing that is perplexing you?

Projects Often Take More Time than a Single Cycle Round

You could go through a cycle of Flow, Production, Organization and Rest phases and not complete your project. Big projects often take time. In that time you may cycle through the four phases multiple times. Because of the ebbs and flows of energy and interest, it's easy to forget your projects or lose enthusiasm for them along the way. If a project is important to you, you won't want it to get lost in the process. It's incredibly easy to never complete projects if you aren't careful.

Keep track of your projects and come back around to the project you haven't finished. It's amazing how easily you can forget that you even had a project after you've been through the apathy and boredom of the Rest phase. You could totally forget what you were working on last month. Find an accountability partner or coach who will help you remember what you were doing and bring you back to it. You may feel you've lost enthusiasm for the idea. It may be that the timing is off and you need to back burner that idea. On the other hand, if you will at least try to come back to task on your latest project, it probably won't be as boring as you thought it would be. You can dig deeper into it. You can find new ideas within it. It can be rich and alive, a fun place to explore with your creativity and inspirational hardwiring.

I often have two or three projects that I'm working on. When I hit a Flow state, I look at those projects and pick up the one that's resonating with me. It's often like I'm moving several balls forward at once. It's better to choose something than to do nothing. If you waste the Flow state in indecision, you'll have nothing to work on in the Production stage. You'll just flounder. Find your focus and stick with it.

Conquering Indecision

One of the biggest time wasters is indecision. We have trouble making decisions because we lack clarity about who we are and what our overall purpose is.

Clarity gives you direction. Direction enables you to make faster decisions. Faster decisions allow you to take advantage of the Production state that follows Flow.

To gain an overall clarity about your purpose and direction, I have a worksheet inside my Inspired Creatives course that will help you create your mission statement at www.MarnieKuhns.com/ creatives . You'll also find a video in the course on making faster decisions.

Imagine that you have a storm of ideas raining down while you're in a Flow state. When you have a clear direction for your life and business, you can quickly see which ideas fit and which ones don't. You can toss out the ones that don't fit and narrow your decision to the ones that do.

Once you've narrowed your choices down to three options that are in alignment with your purpose, you can decide which option to implement. Deciding which of those three to implement can depend upon the amount of time, space and resources you have available for implementation.

For example, a gardener may choose from hundreds of seeds to plant. How does he know which ones to put in the ground? He looks at several things in making that decision:

- How much garden space do I have?
- How much time do I have in my growing season?
- How long does it take this seed to grow? Do I have enough time to grow it?
- Will this seed grow in my soil? Do I have the right kind of climate for it?
- Is the timing right? Is it the right season for the seed to grow?
- Personal preference. Will my family and I enjoy this fruit or vegetable or flower?

If you have an idea, you can run it through a similar series of questions.

- Do I have space for this idea? Do I have room in my life for it? For example, early on in my business, I knew I wanted to be a speaker, but I had small children at home. Traveling wasn't a viable option. As my children got older, traveling and speaking became easier to do. I now have space for this idea which I didn't have before.
- How much time do I have right now for this idea? If you're taking care of an ailing elderly parent, now might not be the time for you to start a large time-intensive project.

- How long will it take to get this idea to completion? Do I have that kind of time available to wait for a harvest? For example, do you need the money immediately to pay your house payment? If so, an idea that could take a year to produce revenue wouldn't be your first choice. (Not to say it wouldn't be wise to have something long range in the works.)
- Do I have the right systems in place or business model for this idea?
- Do I have the skill set, the energy, and the resources?
- Am I going to get bored with this idea? If so, why? Do I have the money to hire the people who do have the skill set or temperament for the project?
- Is the timing right? Let's say it's the heat of the summer and you want to grow broccoli. You probably won't have much luck since broccoli grows better in cooler weather. I've had many ideas over the years that I had to set aside until the timing was right. For example, I wanted to write a book distilling the laws of freedom my father taught me for nearly 20 years before the time was finally right to write it. Over those 20 years there was hardly any public interest in the topic. But when the world needed it, I had already thought through and discussed with my father much of what I wanted to include. Because of this, the writing took very little time.
- Will I enjoy implementing this idea? Does it feel right? Is it going to make me happy?

Let's say you have an idea that doesn't meet one or more of the criteria above. You don't have to toss it; you can put it on the back burner to simmer a bit. Put it on your master list of ideas until the resources, time, and energy are available.

An important question to ask yourself in business is: "Does this idea need to produce revenue? If so, how quickly do I need to produce revenue from this idea?" If you need money from it immediately, choose an idea that can be implemented and brought to market quickly. If money isn't pressing, you can work on ideas that take longer to implement. Years ago, money was more of a pressing concern for me, so I selected ideas that would generate revenue in a few weeks to a couple of months. I call these types of ideas "early harvest crops." They produce results quickly, but they might burn out quickly, too.

As money isn't an issue for me at present, I focus on a lot of projects that will take longer to gestate but which have potential to produce ongoing revenue down the road. I call these "late harvest crops." For example, some types of corn are late harvest. Their gestational periods are longer. Let's say you have an idea that may take two-three years to generate revenue, go ahead and start it in motion — especially if you have the time, space and resources to take a few steps forward on it.

I've done this with many ideas and projects. As I said earlier, I usually have multiple projects going and pick the one that I'm in the mood to work on when I reach a Flow state. These projects could all be at different phases of production. It's like planting a mix of early harvest and late harvest crops.

As I mentioned earlier, some ideas are like fruit trees. They take three-five years to bear fruit, so you want to go ahead and plant them. They don't take a lot of energy. You put them in the ground, make sure they're protected and have water. Overall, they aren't high maintenance, but 3-5 years down the road, they can bring you a continual ongoing harvest. So, think ahead with your seeds. Don't get so wrapped up in "I have to have money right now," that you neglect planting some late harvest crops as well. You need those to start stabilizing your cash flow.

Here's an example: Years ago, my husband was good friends with a dairy farmer in central Wisconsin. The friend had hundreds of acres of beautiful pasture and fields, but he also had several acres of rocky hills that were impossible to farm.

My husband hunted on those rocky hills. One day, my husband told the farmer, if he wanted, he would bring over some black walnuts and help him plant them. And they did.

Fast forward three decades later. The dairy farmer still owns the property but leases it out for annual crops (mostly soybeans and corn). He gets some income off that, and he and his wife work in a nearby city. My husband went out to visit the old farm. As he greeted his friend, he looked towards some of the rocky hills.

The black walnut trees, dozens of them, are large, stately trees producing walnuts like crazy. More importantly, they are now large enough to harvest for timber and sell to local mills. Each tree is worth between $15,000 and $25,000. With dozens of trees on the property ... you get the picture. The dairy farm was an early harvest crop. It provided immediate financial stability. The black walnut trees are a late harvest crop.

In another example, IdeaMarketers.com was both a long-term and a short-term producer for me. It took a lot of time and energy over the years. Usually it ran smoothly and required little effort for months on end. But if I launched a new revenue stream inside the site — that could be time intensive. Other times the site needed a face-lift and required a lot of effort to remodel. Once it was well established, it got lots of traffic, and became a wonderful advertising revenue source. That required very little effort on my part and provided a consistent cash flow — whether I was working or not. This is an example of a fruit tree or late harvest crop.

When you have fruit trees in place in your business, you don't have to work like crazy all the time. You don't get caught in the "create it, launch it, create it" cycle trap.

The more ongoing revenue streams you can create the better. You want a mix of both early and late-harvest revenue streams. It's up to you to look at your pressing needs and decide where to put your focus.

Eventually, you'll spend less time on the create-it-launch-it hamster wheel and more time watering and feeding your late harvest and perennial crops.

Building Relationship Capital

For example, the time spent building relationships in the real world and on social media, writing blogs, and creating content all go into the fruit tree I call "Relationship Capital."

Building rapport with people is a late harvest crop. Relationships are worth gold. They pay and they keep on paying. You don't always see immediate fruit, though. Businesses, families and collaborate relationships are late harvest crops and you must trust that one day they are going to bear fruit. Keep feeding them with positive energy.

You may launch two or three early harvest revenue streams in a year, but always feed your late harvest crops. Build relationships, market consistently, advertise and drive traffic to your business so your passive revenue stays steady and increases. As I mentioned earlier, my business didn't really take off until I hired a friend and delegated the ongoing, every-day tasks that continually fed my late harvest and perennial crops.

When you think about your idea seeds, don't get frustrated when you don't have the time or resources to make them happen. You may not have everything in your soil to make an idea grow. If you've taken the time to build relationship capital, a colleague might step in and bridge the gap. For example, I'm never going to be a person of meticulous routines and consistency, but I've hired and joint ventured with people who are.

If your soil is missing something, you can get an additive to enrich it. That requires being honest enough with yourself to acknowledge your weaknesses and bring in other people to fill those gaps. This can be done with joint ventures, bartering, subcontracting and hiring. That's why building relationship capital is so important!

The Power of Writing Things Down

Suppose you're implementing these concepts. You've gotten clear on the overall objective for your life and business. You've analyzed your ideas based on how soon you need to generate revenue and the resources, time and energy you have available to invest.

You've narrowed down three ideas that fit the best. You've selected one that you're going to act on now while you're feeling a burst of productive energy. The other two align and you love them, but you don't have the time, energy or resources for them.

Don't throw them away. Put them on your master list. Doing so is like putting seeds in the ground. You'll be amazed at what happens when you do this with your ideas.

Write your ideas down. I once found an old list when I was cleaning my office. On the list was a goal to write a book that was sold on the shelves of a specific bookstore. The list got filed away in a cabinet, and I didn't think about it. By the time I found the list again years later, the goal had been accomplished. Today I've had several of my books sold in that bookstore.

Write your ideas down! Writing them is part of "planting them." If the time, resources and energy aren't available now, one day they will be. Trust that it will happen in a very organic, natural way that is for your highest good. Don't try to force things outside their time or season. Let them happen naturally by taking what actions you can and trusting the pathway will materialize for you in the perfect time and way.

Have you had an idea that you weren't ready to implement, but wrote it down, and found that the people and resources started gathering?

Affirmations

I'm a big believer in the power of affirmations. They help you retrain your brain to think positively about things. They also help remove unproductive thoughts. Here are some ideas for affirmations you can use as an inspired creative.

- I finish ideas that are in my highest good to finish
- I can learn the business skills I need to be successful
- I can say "no" to people and still be a nice person
- Saying "no" to what's outside my focus opens space for more possibilities within my pivot point
- I make good decisions quickly and easily

- It's safe for me to make decisions quickly
- I trust my intuition
- It's safe for me to trust my intuition
- I have good discernment
- It's safe to trust my discernment
- When there looks like there's no way out, a way will unfold
- I adapt as necessary
- Change is a good thing
- I am an evolving, progressing being
- I adapt and adjust quickly as necessary
- I am the creator of my own life
- God is ok with my creating my own life and He'll help me do it wisely
- I believe in myself
- I believe in my message
- People need what I have to offer
- There is a place in the world for me and my message
- All the resources, people and money I need come to me as I need it
- I trust my creative cycle
- I work with my creative cycle
- I let go of the need to be inspired around people to fit in
- I let go of the need to inspire other people to fit in / to hold value
- I fit in
- I stand up for myself and still fit in
- I stand up for myself and people like me
- I speak my truth and people like me
- I make room for my creativity
- I release the need for everyone to like or agree with me
- I let go of the need to inspire others to fit in
- I let go of the need to be inspired to fit in
- I know what I want and I go for it

- I know what I need to do next
- I have a space for my creativity
- I can stick with a task until completion
- I am focused
- I am connected with the infinite flow of money
- I am clear on my direction
- All the resources, people and money I need comes to me when I need it
- I let go of neediness
- Abundance flows in and through me freely

Timeless Marketing Methods

Having been in business since the inception of the Web, I have seen big changes in how things work. I survived the dot com bust. I survived Google's Panda update. I've transitioned the period where there were large content websites that have been replaced with social media giants. I remember when, in the early days of the Internet, people's lives didn't revolve around their smart phones or communicating instantly through social media platforms. You went to the Internet when you wanted to look something up or check your email. Today, we panic if we can't get an internet connection.

Obviously, what worked in marketing a decade ago doesn't work today. Things are always changing. But there are some things that are timeless. I'd like to share with you some guidelines about marketing that hopefully will help you regardless of the latest technology or the latest fads. They worked when I started out in business and they still work today.

Be Real. Be You. Be Vulnerable

In whatever industry you're in, there are probably thousands of other people doing the same thing. What makes you unique is you. Your personal interests, your core values, your unique voice, your way of relating to people are all important. These things are what make you stand out.

The people who resonate with you will hire you. Be willing to get vulnerable. When I went through the simultaneous deaths of my mother and my marriage, I became vocal on Facebook about what I was dealing with. I didn't drag anyone through the mud, but I talked about how it felt, what it was like for me, what I was doing to cope. People were reading my posts more than ever before. They were responding, telling me that my posts were so helpful because they were going through something similar. I gave people words for the feelings they couldn't quite articulate. Having someone put their feelings into words meant a lot to them.

I've been offering free 20-minute consults for years. People might talk with me about business, marketing, life or whatever. People would schedule appointments during this time period and tell me about how they lost their dad recently or how they'd been through a tough divorce and that what I wrote really meant something to them. Then they'd say something like, "So I need someone to help me with my Facebook Ad Management. Tell me about what you can do for me."

My life experiences were completely unrelated to Facebook Ad Management, yet it connected in the prospect's mind. They wanted someone managing their Facebook ads that they knew, liked, and felt they could trust.

Back in the beginning of my business when the Web wasn't a part of our daily lives, the businesses that hired me did so primarily because of word of mouth. I helped a woman learn a software package. She got a job at Coca-Cola and recommended me to the VP of Sales and Marketing. He brought me in for a conversation. He liked me and gave me a job programming a case sales tracking system. The project was a success. The system increased his efficiencies and helped Coca-Cola sell more products. This made the VP look good and he was a fan. That gentleman became a friend and we stayed in contact for years. In time, he referred me to other businesses he worked with.

That's just one example of the power of relationship, of being yourself, of being likeable. I built my computer consulting practice purely on relationship.

Don't Put All Your Eggs in One Basket

Make sure you're reaching people through multiple platforms. I know business owners who still haven't recovered from the demise of article marketing. It was the main way they generated traffic and thus sales. When Google began punishing the content directories, it hurt a lot more people than just the content directories.

This is an important lesson to learn. Don't just focus on your Facebook likes or your Twitter followers or your LinkedIn profile or your Pinterest boards. Even though email is relatively passé, build an email list anyway. At least you own that and can back it up. You can carry it to a new list manager if the one you're using goes belly up or stops functioning properly.

You don't own your Facebook, Twitter or LinkedIn followers. If one of these platforms decides they don't like you and locks you out of your account, you're toast if they're your only means of reaching people.

A good old-fashioned database of your customers, their addresses, phone numbers and emails should not be overlooked. Find ways to collect that information. And for heaven's sake, back it up! Don't count on your email or online shopping system to always be there. Companies go out of business. Online services can get hacked.

Keep multiple backups on and off the cloud and in a fireproof box. If you really want to be safe, print them out and put them in a fireproof box. If you're delegating, don't give one individual control over your database. Make sure you have the logins for all your accounts and that you're making your own periodic backups. I have a client who lost a database of 30 million email addresses because the relationship with the person managing his database went sour. He literally had to start over from scratch!

Use multiple methods of contacting people. Good old-fashioned snail mail and a personal phone call could make the difference between someone hiring you over hiring someone else. If your business warrants, consider building a texting database. Currently, more people look at their texts than they do nearly any other method of communication. Just don't abuse it. Remember, too much of a good thing is not a good thing.

Think of as many ways as you can to reach your audience. You don't have to be everywhere. You just want to be where your customers are.

Be Consistent

Whatever platforms or methods you decide to use to reach your prospects and clients, be consistent. Consistency pays huge dividends. You want people to feel like they see you everywhere. They used to say it took seven interactions before someone bought from you. Nowadays I've heard people say it takes 21. Whatever the number, it takes a lot. Consistency matters. I'm not talking about pestering people. I'm talking about offering consistent valuable content and resources.

If consistency isn't your strong suit, delegate it or use an automated service to create consistency with your outreach.

Pay Attention to Your Numbers

Marketing is about testing, tweaking and tracking. A simple change in a headline could increase your sales from non-existent to a screaming success. But if you don't test, tweak and track you could miss out on sales that are right under your nose. One small change could make all the difference. But if you make those changes without recording and monitoring what you're doing, you could completely miss what's happening.

Back when I first started out in business, I read a book called "Ogilvy on Advertising." The principles taught in it are timeless. Get a copy. Study it.

Ogilvy talks about how you only change one thing at a time and keep records. Back when IdeaMarketers,com was making four figures a month in ad revenue from Google Adsense™ revenues, I read about a different way to place the ads on the page to get better results. I decided to test the theory. I made a simple change to the article template page which made millions of articles show up with the new ad placement. My revenues jumped from four figures to five figures a month as a result.

One small change, 15 minutes, and crazy profitable results.

If I'd made too many changes at once I wouldn't have been able to pinpoint what caused the jump.

Be willing to try new things. Make changes, log and track the results of those changes. A colleague once told me that she tells her clients that until they have tried something seven different ways, they can't tell her that a business idea won't work.

Just because something doesn't work the first time doesn't mean it's a bad idea. You may just need to tweak how you explain it, how you're selling it, a headline, a sales page, or the ad you're using.

When you track, pay attention to where the breakdown is. For example, when I run Facebook ads for clients, if the ads I create are getting the client great traffic to their opt-in page for a good price, but people aren't filling out the form for the offer, then I know it's the offer page that's the problem. Maybe that page needs a new headline. If the client changes the headline and their opt-in rate increases, we know we've got that much right. Then, if people are opting in for the free offer, but aren't buying, we know there's a breakdown in the upsell process somewhere. The follow-up emails may need tweaking. If people are reading the emails and clicking through to the sales page, but sales aren't happening, then we know the sales page has the problem.

You can't market effectively if you don't track. And you can't succeed if you don't test, tweak and try new things!

Be Responsive and Communicate

Even though the Internet has greatly expanded our ability to communicate, very few of us use it the way we should. I don't know many online businesses that take the time to pick up the phone and thank a customer for an order.

If you subscribe to a monthly service, you get the monthly charge to your card, but how many times do you hear from the company throughout the month? It's human nature to lay low and hope customers forget that they're paying you $9, $27, or $99 per month for a service.

I know I've been guilty of not wanting to rock the boat. If someone was paying me $200/month for our expert promotion and we were doing the work, if I didn't hear from that expert, I'd assume all was well. But occasionally, I'd remind myself that wasn't the right way to do business. I'd pick up the phone or shoot the person a personal email and ask them how things were going. I'd ask if there was something they'd like us to promote for them.

I've found that a little bit of personal communication goes a long way.

For example, when someone buys one of my programs, if they provide a phone number, I like to surprise them with a call and thank them for their order. I don't do it every time, but I have been known to do it frequently.

I've found that my best ideas for new products and services come from picking up the phone and calling an old customer or an existing one. It's not a survey. It's not a sales pitch. There's nothing scripted. It's just a "Hi! How are you doing? What are you up to these days? Is there anything I can do for you?" type of call.

People appreciate the personal touch. They often give me ideas for improving my offerings or an idea for something completely new I'd never thought of.

For example, when IdeaMarketers was in its infancy, someone suggested it would be cool if they could mark the articles that they wanted to use in their newsletters or ezines for later reference. I took the idea, added to it and created a newsletter builder. The newsletter builder created their newsletter for them. They selected the articles they wanted in a shopping-cart style system, added any custom information they wanted, selected a template and it built their newsletter for them. They could just copy it into their email program and send it.

Then, people asked if they could save time and not have to request permission to use articles. I gave the writers a checkbox where they could give people pre-authorized use if they were using the newsletter builder. The person reprinting the article agreed to use the person's name and resource box when the article was reprinted. The newsletter builder then showed pre-authorized articles at the top of searches so they could quickly create their newsletters without having to stop and ask permission for most of the articles.

Responsiveness Can Lead to More Business

It's important to be responsive when people reach out to ask for advice. Recently, one of my clients who hadn't booked a session for a while messaged me on Facebook to ask for some parenting advice. I chatted with her a bit, giving her some ideas. A couple hours later, I noticed she'd ordered a SimplyHealed™ session with me. I dropped her another instant message and thanked her for booking. She simply said, "I haven't had a session in a while."

Being willing to "be there" for her without trying to upsell her in any way led to a sale.

Offer Update Reports

I've also noticed that people like reports. If you're offering a service to a client such as marketing, advertising, social media writing or bookkeeping, send your clients periodic reports on what you're doing for them. They love that. A customer who is communicated with is generally a happy customer.

You may think if you just lay low and say nothing, that no news is good news, but you're more likely to lose a customer who doesn't hear from you. If you do make that call and the person says, "By the way, I've been meaning to call you and cancel my subscription," one of two things will happen:

- First, you can apply some TLC and fix the reason they were thinking of cancelling so they stay with you.
- Or second, you can let them go on good terms. Sometimes people's lives change; their businesses are struggling, and they can't afford what you're offering anymore. If you are compassionate and caring and have reached out to them, you've kept a bridge intact. They're more likely to refer you to others and possibly come back and buy from you when things turn around.

Handling Negative Feedback

With 200,000 writers loading content into IdeaMarketers, there were always critical emails coming in about something or another. If the site timed out, people would report that. If their web browser didn't like a page on the site, they sent an email. Some people emailed to say they couldn't figure something out. Some people cussed me out over something they didn't like. There were positive comments too. But bottom line, there were lots of emails to wade through daily.

Responsiveness became a priority for me. Occasionally, I had people who were completely floored that I answered emails myself... that I added that personal touch. Yes, I had a virtual assistant who helped with many aspects of the site, but I liked keeping my finger on the pulse of what people were saying.

Some of my very best ideas for improvements on the site came from complaints.

For example, when you have a huge website, navigation is crucial. If someone can't find something, they will just leave your site. Whenever someone complained that they couldn't find a function on IdeaMarketers, I would put it in a more prominent location so it could easily be found. One of the biggest improvements I made in the site was letting my daughter (who has a web design degree and excellent organizational skills) take a look at my site and rethink the entire menu system, making it more intuitive for people to find things.

Here's how I learned to handle negative feedback.

- First, see if what the person is saying is valid. Is there really a problem that needs to be fixed?
- If so, fix it and thank them for bringing it to your attention. If there's no real problem, thank them anyway and move along.
- If someone cusses you out, hit the delete key and don't respond. Every rude email does not need to be responded to. Nobody said you must take abuse.
- If people keep asking you for something, perhaps there's a new product or service idea there. Get to work on creating it!

You don't have to have a huge content site to follow this advice. It can work for any business. Businesses are about relationships – relationships with your customers, your employees, your subcontractors, and your joint venture partners.

Let People Know You Care

One afternoon when I was in the middle of an Amazon Bestseller Launch for my Trust Your Heart: Building Relationships That Build Your Business book, I was feeling pretty burnt out. I had a massive stress headache. Amazon book launches can be quite intensive – especially ones where you've got two dozen contributors you're coordinating and communicating with on launch day.

The book was doing well and climbing the charts. I was experiencing what I'd call good stress. Even good things are stressful sometimes and I needed some fresh air.

I went outside and began walking around our property. It was a gorgeous day: blue skies, spring day, perfect temperature and a gentle breeze. The glory of the day made me feel intensely grateful. I began praying in my mind, thanking God for such a gorgeous day and the successes of it.

Before long I felt relaxed, at peace, whole, and healed of the stress headache I had ten minutes earlier.

At that moment, I realized that all of nature was broadcasting a very simple message:

• I love you.
• Come to me.
• I can heal you.
• I love you.
• Come to me.
• I can heal you.

Nature made good on its promise. I felt healed. Any time I'm stressed, if I go to her, nature delivers.

As I thought about this message, I thought about my own desire to deliver positive messages to the world. I've spent decades trying to cut through the noise and put good things into the world.

That afternoon, I considered that my quest to deliver messages might be as simple as nature's.

What if I let people know I loved them (cared about them), that they were important and then invited them to come to me because I had a solution that could heal them?

Simple Solutions

In business, we're all basically offering solutions – or at least we should be. A new dress offers a solution. It may be that it makes the woman wearing it feel better about herself. Or maybe it makes her feel comfortable or classy or in style. Maybe it keeps her warm. Whatever the reason, it's solving a problem.

If we want people to come to us and listen to or purchase the solutions we offer, we first need to let them know we care!

When you approach marketing from a place of love and caring for people – when you put people and their needs and concerns before the money – people respond. What's more, your marketing can become easy, natural and fun. As you focus on helping people and focusing on them, your marketing becomes more effective and more natural.

At the root, business and marketing are about building relationships. In the next section we'll explore how to harness the power of relationships in your business in a way that few people ever do.

Tap Into Infinite Resources with Quantum Collaboration

You have something important to share with the world. How do I know that? Because if you're someone who is concerned with having a Spirit-led business, your heart and mind are focused on being a part of something significant and worthwhile. You're someone who isn't content to do the same old thing day after day after day. You realize that the "old model" (as some call it) isn't working anymore. You sense that there is something bigger and grander awaiting you as you step out with purpose and serve those you're on this planet to serve.

It's true. You can and will do great things — to the extent that you realize you can't do it alone. As entrepreneurs, we often suffer from the "lone wolf" syndrome. We think we must do everything ourselves. I was this way when I first started my business. I felt everything was up to me and I worked 60-70 hour weeks in my business. I slept, ate, drank and talked business. Even when I wasn't "working," I was still thinking about work, trying to come up with solutions for problems I didn't even know existed yet. I didn't know who I was outside of my work.

Did it help? Did it make me rich? No, it made me tired, overwhelmed and irritable. Not until I started following my passion, working with my strengths, delegating, and forming collaborative relationships, did my business start to take off. As it did, I became happier and healthier.

As Spirit-led entrepreneurs, we can make a difference in the world around us. But until and unless we learn to work collaboratively with others, we won't create the impact we're capable of making on the world.

I frequently visit a building with a huge chandelier. The bottom of it is cone shaped and the top is a pillar that extends from the cone, up into the ceiling heavenward. The first time I visited this building I loved the white light extending out from the mass of crystal to fill the room. The second time I was there, I was able to sit close to the chandelier, a little bit under it. The more I looked up at it, I noticed all the colors coming from it (red, orange, yellow, green, blue, indigo and violet), thousands of points of light emanating from the sea of crystal.

As I studied closely, I noticed that all of the light was coming from one main light source at the top that shone down into the center of the chandelier. As the light refracted through these thousands of prisms, it created stars of brilliant, colorful light. Then I noticed that the interior decorators had positioned this chandelier between two facing mirrors. On each opposing wall was a mirror, directly aligned and facing each other, with the chandelier in between. It created a sense of infinity. The reflection kept going on and on in a corridor of eternity.

I sat there for some time and pondered on how we are a lot like the prisms within this chandelier. As we combine our efforts, we are like the chandelier itself.

When we choose to join with others to magnify the light, we magnify our influence. Our impact reverberates throughout eternity. If you thought you had to light the world by yourself as an individual prism, that would be daunting and overwhelming, wouldn't it? But if you join with others, you can create this amazing light source that leads heavenward, that extends through infinity, that impacts eternity.

This chandelier is a physical symbol of what I call Quantum Collaboration.

Quantum Collaboration is a way of being, a way of interacting with other people. It's a way of harnessing the power of synergy where the sum is equal to or greater than the parts.

The Importance of Being Clear

I was telling a friend about my insights from the chandelier, and she exclaimed, "Oh, I volunteered one time in that building with some other women. Together we cleaned that chandelier." The chandelier was taken down, and the women sat around it on the floor, pulling each individual prism out, cleaning it and replacing it. Periodically this is done because if dust gets on the prisms, the chandelier won't have the illuminating effect.

This is an important aspect of collaboration... each individual crystal must be clean and clear about its function. If we apply this to entrepreneurship, we understand why being very clear about your own pivot point is important. Knowing who you are, why you do what you do, who you serve, and what you deliver is the clarity you need to effectively collaborate. If people don't know what you're about, what your purpose is, they will direct their attention elsewhere. More importantly, they will not be able to participate in your brilliance.

I once interviewed a couple of colleagues who were joint venturing on a significant project together. The pair were so clear about who they are and what they do, that their collaboration was intuitive and seamless. They worked so well together there's almost no need for delegating tasks. They just instinctively are who they are and do what they do best. Combine this with a shared dedication to quality and strong work ethics, and something wonderful happens.

Collaboration

Collaboration is the root of and the key to my success. There's a transference of skills, knowledge and wisdom that happens when you collaborate. Although I went to college for information management, every other skill, knowledge or area of wisdom I've developed over the years has come through collaboration. I've honed programming, writing and marketing skills all through collaboration. The people I collaborated with taught me these things and much more. Their light illuminated me!

As I mentioned earlier, when I started my business, I had no money to hire anyone. I chose the "do it yourself" method, because I had no choice. Through relationships and collaboration, I quickly went from teaching computer software to individuals in a spare bedroom of my home to programming case sales tracking systems for Coca-Cola and large manufacturing concerns – all through the power of relationships.

Here are a few things that have come to me through collaboration and synergistic friendships that I did not have to pay cash for:

- Professional branding and rebranding consulting
- Disney tickets for the whole family
- Web design and graphics work
- Instruction on web design and programming
- New clients, referrals, leads
- Free sales and marketing advice
- The underlying programming code for IdeaMarketers was given to me by my friend and business partner who taught me how to adapt the code for my needs. This saved me months of programming and learning time. I didn't have to pay to take a class. I didn't have to hire a programmer.
- Private mentoring on abundance that in time multiplied my revenue 7-fold.
- A friend and I once generated $40,000 in a month through collaboration and repeated

it for the next 3 months. We split the revenues with the collaborators and helped a lot of people through the dot com bust.

- Therapy from a licensed psychologist when I was going through divorce.
- Private tutoring on creative writing and editing from a university professor.
- Private instruction on copywriting, including re-writes of my copy, critiques of my copy, and even complete sales pages and emails written for me.
- A round table of experts who'd brainstorm with me on virtually any idea I come up with as needed.
- Professional advice on structuring and optimizing group coaching and mentoring.
- Amazing insights from gifted visionaries who've helped me along my spiritual path through vision maps, private readings, guided meditations, energy clearings, and more.
- Assistance at my events – people who manned book sales tables, brought refreshments, found locations for the events.
- Multiple #1 Amazon bestsellers and #1 Amazon Movers and Shakers, and a Barnes and Noble bestseller
- Private coaching and product development advice.
- My take at a single event with about 60 people attending was $4,000 on a collaborative product we sold.
- A team of people who gathered around me with professional advice, support and encouragement when I took the biggest leap ever in my business.

- Opportunities to be a guest speaker and sell my products.

That's just the tip of the iceberg. Would you like to know how to do the same type of thing yourself? You can. It will require thinking a little differently, perhaps shifting a few beliefs you have about the way the world works. And there are a few principles to learn. You might have to reach outside your comfort zone a bit too. But I can teach you how.

I'll be honest with you, I have been hesitant to teach Quantum Collaboration because when you undertake to dissect something that originates from the heart, you dehumanize it. It becomes calculated and more about the "getting" than it is about the spirit of giving. And it is the spirit of giving which underpins Quantum Collaboration.

Quantum Collaboration is not about how to get whatever you want from people, how to manipulate them into helping you when you need it, or making them feel like they "owe you." It's also not about the typical reciprocity, barter-style relationships that many refer to as synergistic or collaborative. It's not about keeping score. In fact, if you keep score, it doesn't work.

If it becomes in the least about what you can "get" from someone else, that person will sense it, and your relationship will be undermined.

Principle #1: Love

At the root of Quantum Collaboration is love. There are others who have written about love – Og Mandino, Marianne Williamson, God! I doubt I could improve upon any of them. If I tell you that in order to engage in Quantum Collaboration you must love everyone, that probably seems impossible. So, what I will attempt to do is dissect what I mean by love. I'm not talking about romantic love, of course. I'm not talking about looking at others through rose-colored glasses, putting them on pedestals, or secreting mega-doses of dopamine into your bloodstream. Although, sometimes I'm downright giddy when I find a potential new collaborative partner. Something's running through my veins!

It comes down to the way we think and feel about the people we meet. Og Mandino in "The Greatest Salesman in the World" suggested the following:

> "And how will I confront each whom
> I meet? In only one way. In silence
> and to myself I will address him and
> say I Love You. Though spoken in
> silence these words will shine in my
> eyes, unwrinkle my brow, bring a
> smile to my lips, and echo in my
> voice; and his heart will be opened.
> And who is there who will say nay to
> my goods when his heart feels my
> love?"

While I don't think the words, "I love you," when I meet a new person, I do think other thoughts, which to me are the essence of love. I approach each person I meet believing that there is greatness within them. It is my quest to locate that greatness. Once found, I enjoy articulating it back to the person. At this point, the person knows that I really "see her." I understand her. I "get" what makes her tick. Most of the time people are amazed because before this point, they couldn't have articulated the greatness within themselves. They may have been completely oblivious to it, and my pointing it out to them is a priceless gift, a present from me to them.

Others may know their greatness but have so few people who really "get them," that to find a stranger who sees them for who they are at the core is a rarity. It reaches in and touches their hearts.

In my experience, it's very difficult to see the greatness in yourself. Therefore, there isn't a more powerful way to express love to someone than to truly see them, recognize them, and articulate their greatness.

To me, this is the essence of love. You may disagree. Love may mean something else to you, and that is fine. But I guarantee you that if you see the greatness in someone and then articulate it back to them, they will instantly find themselves endeared to you. If you go a step further and share the greatness you see in them with others, you have created a solid foundation for friendship.

Again, from Og Mandino's, "The Greatest Salesman in the World:"

> "And how will I speak? I will laud my enemies and they will become friends; I will encourage my friends and they will become brothers. Al-

ways will I dig for reasons to ap-
plaud; never will I scratch for excuses
to gossip. When I am tempted to
criticize, I will bite on my tongue;
when I am moved to praise, I will
shout from the roofs.

"Is it not so that birds, the wind, the
sea and all nature speak with the
music of praise for their creator?
Cannot I speak with the same music
to his children? Henceforth will I
remember this secret and it will
change my life.

"I will greet this day with love in my
heart."

"And how will I act? I will love all
manners of men for each has qualities
to be admired even though they be
hidden. With love I will tear down
the wall of suspicion and hate which
they have built around their hearts
and in its place will I build bridges so
that my love may enter their souls."

When you sincerely value and praise others, it
endears them to you. It can't help but do so.

To illustrate how well this works, I once had a
book critic who praised me in one sentence and
then ripped my writing style to shreds in the
next. She did this in a public forum of both my
peers and a reading audience. I was upset. But
her comments made me seek professional editing
help, and I ended up connecting with a very

talented editor who taught me the rules of good writing.

Several months later, I ran into the book critic at an event and thanked her for her review. I explained to her how it made me realize I needed help and that I wouldn't have found such a fantastic editor friend had it not been for this critic's review. You could tell by the look on her face that she wasn't used to getting this type of response from people she'd publicly criticized. Every time I saw that woman in the future, she held me in the highest regard and always treated me with a great deal of respect. And when she ended up reviewing my next two books, they were very favorable reviews.

Yes, my writing had improved, but also the typical negative comments she always managed to work into any review were conspicuously missing from mine.

Principle #2: Engage

Be present. Interact. Join in. (This is something I had to learn, since I was very shy as a child.) Engaging doesn't always mean engaging your mouth. It means engaging your eyes and ears – listening to the people around you, watching them, observing their gifts, their talents and their skills.

As you do this, you aren't looking at them to compare yourself to them. You aren't looking to find ways you're superior. It's not a contest. Nor are you looking for ways you don't measure up to their level.

For several years, I conducted short 15-minute free consults at a business conference in Atlanta. I'll dissect what I did in those consults to illustrate how I process and filter relationships.

When someone sits across from me for 15 minutes, those 15 minutes are about them. They aren't about me. I'm going to share with you the process I use with these folks because this method of connecting with people is what enables me to collaborate on the level that I do.

- First, I'm on the lookout for greatness. I'm looking for things to admire in this person. I work from the assumption that there is greatness here, and my quest in the next few minutes is to find it.
- Second, I'm listening, looking for ways that I may be of service to them. How can I help them find the next piece to their puzzle? How can I assist them through, over or around whatever's standing in the way of them becoming their highest, best selves? Of achieving their vision?
- Third, I'm looking for ways they may fit into my big vision.
- Fourth, I'm looking for ways they could be of service to anyone else I have met.
- I start by asking them to articulate their intention for the consult. What is the question that's on their minds? Some people can't articulate that exactly, so I work toward drawing that out of them. What is it that they want or need?

- Do I know how to fill or answer that need? Do I know anyone else who can fill or answer that need?
- Facilitate introductions. Sometimes I see the woman I'm talking to needs to meet Jane whom I met an hour ago. Jane has her solution. I won't rest until I've facilitated the introduction between the two people.
- I intentionally sit just inside the room where the consults take place, facing the door so I can see into the hallway as people pass. This way when I see someone pass who needs to connect with someone else, I can wave them down or call to them and facilitate the connection.

You'll notice there are several things I'm NOT doing...

I'm not competing with these people. I don't care if they seem to be doing the same thing I'm doing or have the same message as me. I never look at them as competition. On the rare occasion a twinge of something rises in me, I tell it to hush.

A good way to do this is to remember the potential size of your audience. For example: Pretend a young couple starts writing a blog that is the exact same message your blog is about. They quickly become very successful and have more than 50,000 followers on Facebook alone!

You could quickly get jealous and say "Well, I missed my chance!" OR you could do some math: Say: "300,000,000 people in the USA are my potential followers. This couple has 50,000 of those. That means 299,950,000 people are now my potential audience!"

If you got .02% of those people to follow you, you would have nearly 10,000 more followers than the couple you're jealous of! And there's nothing to say that the 50,000 people who follow the young couple would not also follow you.

Each person I meet is a resource, a connection, an extension of me. I may or may not do business with them in the future. They might connect me to another person I need to meet.

I keep a mental file of the people I meet. I honestly don't remember the names of everyone I meet. That's an area in which I could improve. What I do remember are their stories and the experiences I've shared with them.

Principle 3: Experience

The more someone lets me experience what they do, the more likely I can create a collaborative or synergistic relationship with them. Some people I will hire in order to experience them. But some of the most powerful relationships that have come to me have been through mutual exchange. They have what I need, and I have what they need.

This means opening yourself up to learning from other people and articulating where you need help. I have an underlying belief that everyone has something to teach me, and there are some people who can transform your life if you let them.

In 1998, I was promoting a lot of coaches, but I didn't know much about coaching. I belonged to an email discussion group with dozens of other businesswomen. A woman named Jenette in the group was fresh out of coaching university and was looking to gain more experience. She volunteered to coach a handful of people for 3 months. She posted this to the list, and I responded. I wanted to experience coaching to understand it better so I could promote my clients better.

We began working together. By three months in, we realized we had a possibility for some synergy here. I loved what she did and was able to get more done with her holding me accountable. In return, she realized her need for some web work and promotion. We struck a deal. She'd coach me, if I helped her. It was informal. No tit for tat, no retail for retail. Just an "I'll help you, if you help me." It worked.

And what came out of that exchange is one of the most priceless friendships of my life. We literally transformed each other's lives. She's also the one who encouraged me to start SheLovesGod.com.

Remember that story I shared earlier about meeting Leslie Householder through SheLovesGod.com? Do you recall how Leslie went on to teach me principles that multiplied my revenues seven-fold? I would have never met her without Jenette.

Over the years, I can directly connect $1 million in additional revenues in my business back to meeting Leslie Householder and the principles she taught me. Over the years, we've continued to collaborate – putting on events together, cross promoting one another. We also have developed and maintained a wonderful friendship.

It all started with Leslie extending herself – letting me experience her knowledge and wisdom firsthand. She generously, and without strings attached, offered to help me in a way few people on this planet ever would. She made such a profound impact on my life that I consider myself forever in her debt. I'm sure I'll be singing Leslie Householder's praises until the day I die.

With Synergistic Friendships and Collaboration, The Sum Is Greater than the Parts

You never know the phenomenal results you're going to get with collaboration. Through my friendship with Jenette, we both experienced a complete spiritual transformation. Neither of us would ever be the same. The spiritually connected person I am today is a byproduct of this relationship.

She wanted greater connection with God, and as I shared with her what I knew, her life transformed. In the process, I gained a greater appreciation for the truths I knew and began applying them better in my own life. I became more regular in my spiritual practices and this deepened my connection with God. I went from simply knowing things to being converted fully to Christ. We started out in what looked like a simple business exchange and in the process, we gained something infinitely more priceless.

By Leslie opening and sharing her knowledge with me, she set herself on a path that allowed her to package and deliver her knowledge to tens of thousands of people online. Their lives have been affected like mine was. The rippling impact of her generosity has paid off exponentially – not only serving herself and me but thousands of other people as well.

Principle 4: Look for the Connection

Is there a connection? Does the person move you?

Over the years, I've met different individuals who stand out to me. I was a bit of an amateur rock collector growing up. I loved to collect rocks and put them in a rock tumbler, polish them and then mount them as jewelry. I think I'm still doing that in a way – except people are my stones.

In fact, when I meet someone who moves me in this way, I say "I've found another stone." One such individual entered my life after purchasing my *You're Here for a Reason: Discover and Live Your Purpose* book. I gave away a free consult to those who purchased on a specific day. Judy Ranken purchased the book and when we touched base for her 30-minute consult, it transformed into a 3-hour conversation. I instantly had the impression that this woman was special and that I was to do what I could to serve her. We struck up a friendship. I helped her with her web site and getting her book into print. She became a valued spiritual mentor to me. Her work with guided meditations helped me gain a richer, deeper connection with God and helped me acknowledge and embrace my own spiritual abilities. That has led me to help others.

Instead of discounting my intuition, I began proactively listening to it, and the results have been amazing. To say Judy Rankin changed my life would be a gross understatement.

Another one of these "stones" I've collected was a young woman named Martina Muir. She went through my Rejoice in 2007 program. My goal was to help 2007 people in 2007 through a free email coaching program. Martina and I didn't connect personally during the program. She was just on my email list and on some of the calls I did. But in September 2009, she came up to me during the intermission of an event I spoke at and introduced herself. She told me about how she had placed a baby for adoption as a 17-year-old and went on to pilot post placement support programs for birth mothers. She also helped launch and spoke at adoption conferences that were broadcast internationally.

A month later, my friend Leslie Householder was offering a book retreat in Flagstaff, AZ and had a last-minute opening – one of the gals who was supposed to come couldn't make it and Leslie wanted to know if I wanted the spot. This was a Friday afternoon. The retreat started on Monday. I decided within the hour to go, bought my plane ticket and was on a flight to Phoenix Sunday afternoon.

After arriving, Leslie told me that the girl who had to back out had been able to raise the money for the retreat and was coming after all. Guess who the girl was? Martina Muir. Over the course of the week, Martina and I became friends, and I recognized her as one of those individuals I refer to as "one of my stones." In fact, Martina reminded me so much of my friend Judy Rankin, that I asked Leslie if it would be all right to invite Judy to drive down to meet with Martina and share some of her guided meditation with the group. Leslie agreed and Judy hopped in the car and drove five hours to Flagstaff on a moment's notice.

That introduction and Judy's arrival at that retreat would continue to play a role in all three of our lives. I'll share more about that shortly but let me back up a few years first.

I want to tell you about another one of my stones. I was at a bookseller's convention in Utah back in 2004 at my book distributor's booth signing books. Next to me was a young man my distributor represented. Sheldon Pickering is a pianist and he had his CDs there with headphones so you could listen. I experienced Sheldon's music and instantly fell in love with his style.

I had a clear, firm impression and a thought entered my mind with great strength, "Help this young man." I followed the directive and offered to help Sheldon put his music online. He gave me copies of his CDs, and I built him a little web site. I sold some of his Christmas CDs on my site for a time. Eventually, Sheldon and I lost touch, but I continued to listen to and love his music.

In September of 2009, I was staying at Judy Rankin's house. While there, Judy played some of her daughter Jamie Bartchi's violin music for me. I instantly felt a connection. I knew that I wanted to meet this girl, that she and her music were significant.

Then a few months later in December of 2009, when Lisa Rae Preston (one of my IdeaMarketers experts), Judy, and I were hashing out the plans for the *Light the World: Birthing Your Destiny Retreat*, Sheldon came to mind. So did Jamie. I felt God telling me to pull out the stops – to put together my dream event. If I were going to create such an event, I would love to have both Jamie and Sheldon perform. What's more, I knew that if they played together it would create something exceptional.

People Enter Your Life for a Reason

As we went forward planning the Light the World Retreat and promoting it, Martina Muir came back into the picture. She not only attended the event, but also brought several other women with her. We wouldn't have had a fourth of our participants without Martina.

Since that time Martina has gone on to become a powerfully talented energy worker. She's gotten me through some of the roughest spots of my life – including the period when my mother died, and my husband asked for a divorce simultaneously. Most likely I wouldn't be happily married to my wonderful husband today if Martina hadn't given me a place to stay and heal.

I cannot overemphasize the importance of following the Spirit's nudges about people. God is a master matchmaker. He puts people in our lives at the right time and place so we can help them and so they can help us.

Principle 5: Set the Stage

Musicians are probably the best illustration of collaboration.

When I first had the idea of having Jamie and Sheldon perform at this event, I didn't see the full reason for it. It just felt right. It felt fun. As we progressed in putting the event together, I realized that musicians are the ultimate illustration of how to connect and collaborate with others in a synergistic way.

Little did I know, they both would end up adding to the instruction at the event. Sheldon spoke the night he performed on the piano. Jamie became an integral part of the instructor team.

> "In all of my collaborative experience musically, my favorite co-artists are the ones who can sense when to take the lead and when to be the "embellishment." When that give-and-take is intuitive and flowing, the music is the most creative and fun. That's how I felt with Sheldon. And I can easily think of a handful of others

who are similar to play with. I think
part of that ability is a certain level of
musicianship — they can sense the
overall form of the music, like when
it's time for a chorus or a solo, or
when the repetition has been just
right and it's time to add something
new, etc. They also can sense some
music theory aspects, like which
chord is coming next or which non-
chord tone would add just the right
"umph" to a melody line.

Aside from the level of musicianship,
the other part that makes the intuitive collaboration possible is just that,
intuition. I think it takes a little bit of
music in their soul, a talent for it and
an ear for it. That helps a ton too. :)"
– Jamie Bartschi

When you find those people you connect with
intuitively, you can create some amazing things.

Back to setting the stage... Here are a few ideas
for doing that.

- First, have a clear intention for the outcome you intend. At the Light the World
  Retreat, we wanted each woman to come
  away with a clear idea of who she is and
  how she could impact the world for good
  and how she could work alongside others
  to light the world. I knew that in order to
  do this, we needed to create a loving,

supportive, and nonjudgmental environment.

• Second, lift the lid on your thinking. By asking myself, "If I could have anyone I wanted at this event, who would I choose?" the result was the perfect team, the perfect music and the perfect participants. Out of this event came the most amazing music – music that speaks to my soul, that is an auditory soundtrack that takes me back to one of the most amazing accomplishments of my life.

Principle 6: Let Go of the Need to Micromanage or Control

Do you ever get frustrated when things don't go the way you envision them going? Do other people's choices ever throw a monkey wrench into your plans? Do you ever want something more for someone else than they seem to want for themselves?

In my synergistic relationship with my coach Jenette, I learned important lessons about overcoming pride and ego and about respecting other people's freedom to choose and progress at their own pace. I used to see people's potential so clearly, that I used every trick in the book to help them achieve it – including some not-so-savory methods of guilt tripping, manipulation or pushiness.

In time, I learned to let go of the need to push or control others. I've learned to lovingly hold the vision without pushing others toward it. The individual must want it for themselves.

After learning this important lesson, my relationships started to change. I started to back up, see the beauty, but not try to force or micromanage the unfolding of that beauty.

This was driven home to me at the Light the World Event. I had my four instructors, one of whom was Jamie (the violinist) and then there was Sheldon (the pianist). I had a structure and an outline for the event. I had a basic guide for what would be discussed each day. But much of what went on was adjusting to the dynamic of the group, tweaking what we taught to the audience. I'd wake up at 4 a.m. with a pad and pen and start writing what I planned to say the next day.

It wouldn't come to me months before when I tried to get the material together. It came in the moment – after I'd read the audience, connected with them, engaged them, seen their greatness and sensed where they might be stumbling. In those 4 a.m. moments, it came to me.

Or it would come to us at the end of the day as we sat around in the hotel room, discussing what went on and how we could direct the next day's activities.

I remember standing at the back of the room one afternoon, watching the instructors work with the ladies, and feeling this sense that I simply set the stage and the magic unfolded. I knew I wasn't micromanaging this. I'd set the stage, added the players, and it became something magnificent.

I'm not saying that you don't prepare. You prepare... you study, organize, and get ready. Yet, be prepared to adapt in the moment. Let the Spirit pull from your preparations the things people need in the moment.

My nephew Noah's a singer/songwriter. He has played around the Southeast in different bands and venues. When he's going to perform somewhere and he's auditioning a drummer or a keyboardist, he doesn't tell the person how to play. When he catches them playing something, he likes he says, "I like that. Do that again." He said he gets better performance out of people when he lets their creativity run free and then directs them toward the things he wants to hear more of. Many times, what they come up with far surpasses any original idea he may have had.

This is the way I create collaborative groups. I gather the people, put them together with a bit of direction and the group takes a life of its own. It's what I love about collaboration – you can never predict the magnificence of the harmonies, but you can guarantee there will be some beautiful music made – especially when you create an environment that is safe and nonjudgmental.

What if you work alone? You can still use the power of collaborative groups. Don't try to go it alone. Gather a support group around you. You can do this in any combination of the following ways:

- Start a mastermind group
- Join discussion groups
- Collect a few close friends whom you can go to for advice and to brainstorm ideas
- Join a support group.

Principle 7: Release Judgment and Comparison

Principle 7 is probably the most important of all. At the retreat I've been discussing (the *Light the World: Birthing Your Destiny Retreat*) my underlying intention was to create an atmosphere where there was no judgement or comparison.

My goal for that event was to create a loving environment where each woman would come away understanding the beauty of her soul – and know that there was no need to compare herself to anyone else. Each human life holds value. Each is a pearl of great price of infinite worth and none needs to feel inferior to another.

This is a basic underlying belief system necessary for Quantum Collaboration to work. Remember Quantum Collaboration is a way of being. Each person comes to the setting with clarity about who he or she is, what he or she brings, and without a need to judge others or oneself.

Each day of this 4-day event focused on gaining greater personal clarity and releasing whatever stood in the way of being who we came here to be. As you gain clarity and see your own greatness, there is no need to negatively compare yourself to others. You see your own talents, gifts and wisdom as significant and important. As you do this in a group, you see that everyone has greatness within them and that no two people are the same. There is room for each of us in the world. We are designed to complement one another, not compete with one another.

That's the philosophy behind Quantum Collaboration. That was my quest for this event. While judgment and comparison are probably never going to be completely erased, we set the stage and the outcome was magnificent. In this loving, caring, nonjudgmental environment, a collaborative community was born, and it continues to live on and support me to this day.

In summary, here are the 7 principles of Quantum Collaboration

- Love
- Engage
- Experience
- Look for the Connection
- Set the Stage
- Let go of the need to micromanage
- Let go of judgement and comparison

Please understand that when you exchange what you do or create for money, all you get is money. When you Quantum Collaborate, miracles happen. People, opportunities and knowledge align to help you live your purpose. Most of the time you get far more than you expected.

Quantum Collaboration can take many forms. It can look like my relationship with Jenette where we each came away with what we needed in our spiritual growth and business projects. It can look like my relationship with Leslie where she taught me vital truths and I helped her get her website up and her book published. We've gone on to do other projects together and frequently promote each other via social media and to our email lists.

Quantum Collaboration can look like the collaborative book projects I've done. The first two books in the Trust Your Heart Series include chapters written by dozens of other experts. They were more than your typical collaborative books, though. I created a community around each book where participants could communicate with each other and be an active part of the success of the books. I prominently promoted each contributor throughout the entire book launch.

I went a step further with my *Light the World: How Your Brilliance Can Shift the Planet* book. I had a Light the World Facebook group before I ever started writing the book. As I went into the writing process. I put out a call to members of this group for stories. Within 48 hours I had about 9 stories that fit perfectly in my book. I wrote the bulk of the book, but the stories added richness by giving the reader multiple people's examples of the principles taught in the book.

The same Light the World group helped me find the cover photo for the book. They helped me with proofreading and back cover copy. They even helped me with book events after the book was published. They did everything from finding locations for book events, to bringing refreshments, to helping me with the back of room sales. In turn, they were featured prominently in the book and had the benefit of being in a group of like-minded individuals who want to make a positive difference in the world.

Your Turn

Here's your assignment. Find someone that you feel drawn to – someone you'd like to know more about and reach out to them. Perhaps have a phone discussion. If it's a fit, "experience" one another. You go first. Try giving of yourself to serve another like Leslie did me. Or find someone to "practice" on like Jenette did in coaching me.

Your assignment is to offer your services to someone else – let them experience what you do or learn from you in some way. Remember, it's not tit for tat. It's pouring your gifts into a situation with a heart to serve. Seek to really help someone by using all the gifts, wisdom and talents you have to offer. Connect more deeply. Get to know each other and watch what happens.

I will say that you can't always predict from where your return on investments appear. You may help Jane, but Jane may not be the one who helps you. It may be John who appears in your life and gives you what you need next. As the Bible says, "Cast your bread upon the waters and after many days it will return to you."

This reminds me of something that happened to an elderly woman I know. She's the type of person who is always buying little gifts for people and leaving secret Santa gifts for everyone in her apartment complex. Recently she was at the dentist and the hygienist suggested a fluoride treatment that wasn't paid for by her insurance. She said she would have to pass since she could not afford it at that time.

Shortly afterwards, someone came in and told her that everything on her visit was covered. They gave her the treatment and when she signed out, she discovered that an anonymous patient in the next cubicle overheard her say she didn't have money for the treatment. This person left so much money at the front desk that the woman got all of her treatment paid for and had an $89 credit toward her next visit. She was so moved by the situation she began to cry.

She had spent her lifetime doing thoughtful things for other people. To have it come back to her in that moment was very humbling for her.

You can't put good out in the world and not have it return. By law, it must. Open yourself to the possibilities.

Access A Power Beyond Yourself

When I was growing up, my mom offered a standard piece of advice anytime I had a test or a presentation in school. She'd say, "Say a little prayer." I've followed that advice my whole life and I've found it works incredibly well. In fact, it can work miracles.

Whether I'm prepping for a consulting call, about to teach a class, ready to go on stage to speak, or am writing an article or a book, I say a little prayer. I say lots of little prayers, in fact. Countless times I've been listening to a client explain an incredibly difficult challenge in their lives, and I know I'm there to guide them to their answers. I feel a great sense of responsibility to help them in any way I can. As I listen, I have absolutely no idea what to say to this person. Their challenges are often beyond me.

As they're speaking, in my mind I'll say a little prayer and ask for the words or the insights that I need to share with this person. Every time I do this, sometime during the session, something comes to my mind. By the end of our consult, the client feels hopeful, has more clarity, and knows some solid next steps to take in their life or business.

I know, absolutely know, it wasn't me. I was simply the conduit. Being Spirit-led means getting out of the way and letting the Spirit convey to others what needs to come through you.

Whether you're an inventor, run a service-based business, or are a consultant, speaker, teacher, author or gardener, you can work miracles if you allow the Spirit to work through you.

How to Get Inspired Answers

You may be wondering at this point how this works. How do you get answers in the moment you need them? What does it look like or feel like? For me, it comes in strokes of ideas, or a feeling that I just know the answer or what to say. Or perhaps a visual of something or an analogy will come to mind. It might be a word or phrase.

Everyone gets answers differently. It might be a feeling of peace about a situation where you just know everything's going to be alright. Answers can come as a thought that keeps recurring. If you don't feel like you have this ability to receive answers and be led by the Spirit, think again. Everyone has it ... it's just a very delicate process. It can take time and trial and error to learn to distinguish your thoughts from the Spirit's guidance. We must get quiet, listen, ask and act.

For me, I've found it's better to err on the side of acting on little thoughts and ideas. If they are moral and ethical, I act. If you feel like you should say something and you say it, but it isn't useful to the person, it's no big deal. If you feel like you should take the shopping cart back to the rack instead of leaving it in a parking space, do it. What can it hurt? When you feel a nudge to do some small and simple thing, just do it. From small and simple things, great things are brought to pass. In time, you will learn that action leads to more inspiration. And you will learn to distinguish the voice of the Spirit. It will become a friend to you.

Formula for Receiving Inspiration

Are you stuck for an idea? Struggling with a problem? Having trouble finding answers? Not sure what direction to take? I've found gratitude to be the gateway to revelation. When I take the time to count my blessings, and REALLY feel gratitude for them, there's a connection established between me and the heavens.

There's a formula that I use to receive inspiration. I call it HALO over Gratitude:

HALO

———————

Gratitude

(H) Humble yourself.

Realize that, even with all the talent and wisdom
you have, you can do whatever you need to do so
much better if you have God on your side.
Acknowledge your limitations, your humanness.
Acknowledge God's omniscience and
omnipotence. Acknowledge God's ability to help
you, because He desires to help others.

(A) Ask with Expectation of an Answer

Start with a burning question. Get clear on what
you want to know. And expect an answer. Where
there is a question, there is an answer – by law
there is an answer to every question. I
recommend asking when you're in a quiet space,
if you can. Sometimes that's not possible. If you're
in the middle of a consulting call, you probably
can't step away and find a quiet space. But if
you can, go for a walk in nature, meditate, clear
your mind. If you can, get down on your knees.
Asking from a kneeling position is a position of
humility.

I once saw a presentation by a man who had
developed a special type of photography that could
photograph the auras around people. He showed
us a photo he'd taken of a person kneeling in
prayer. There literally was a light coming from
above the person's head, pouring into the crown
of their head. It was incredible.

(L) Listen

Turn off the cell phones, the TV, get off social
media. Just listen. It may take some time. I call

the revelation process God's bread trail. You may get a clue here and a clue there over the course of a period. Many times, answers don't come in a burst of fully formed illumination. They come a piece at time – line upon line, precept upon precept, here a little, there a little. Express gratitude for any clue along the way. Always listen with grateful expectancy, knowing you will receive an answer.

The more you tap into gratitude, the more likely you will hear the voice of God. Nature is one of the best places I've found to tap into gratitude and to listen. It is always broadcasting God's message, after all: "I love you. Come to me. I can heal you."

Express gratitude for what you already know and for what you already have. Feeling the gratitude is critical. This can't be a cerebral exercise only. You need to really feel the love and gratitude.

Invoke gratitude not only at this point in the process, but all through it.

(O) Obey - Act on whatever comes.

Act fast on inspiration. A lot of people miss the window of opportunity because they don't act while the window is open. The Spirit speaks in a timely fashion. Its messages are not to be ignored. If you don't act, you may not get the next message you need.

Don't dawdle unless you're told to be still and wait for the right moment. Utilize gratitude here. Know that God is going to give you the courage to act and that you know what you need to be doing. When you know that God is in charge, it's easy to lose fear and just go do His will.

(G) Gratitude

The reason I say HALO over Gratitude is because you need gratitude throughout the entire process – while you're asking, while you're listening, while you're acting, after the answers come, and when the results materialize. A grateful heart receives more.

An example of this formula at work happened for me back in September 2009. I had been invited to come out to Utah to be a part of the Women's Information Network Launch. When I was invited, I knew I needed to go. I also knew that I needed to go to Utah for several other things – like meeting my friend Judy Rankin in person for the first time.

Right as the time for the trip approached, we had some immense flooding in Georgia – from where I live in Northwest Georgia all the way down into Atlanta. We live on hill. We have a half-mile gravel driveway that cuts through a field — which is in the floodplain — and goes up a hill to where our house is. That field became a lake on Sunday night. When that happened, I knew we wouldn't get out for three or four days. I knew I would miss my flight Wednesday morning if I didn't get out.

Sunday night we found out at ten o'clock that we would be flooded, but I hadn't packed. I didn't have things ready. I prayed about what to do and felt a feeling of peace that it was going to be okay. I felt like I should pack my bags and go out the next morning (Monday morning).

But by Monday morning, it was already flooded. There was no way to drive out. I checked different ways to get out and couldn't find anything. My brother-in-law, who had gone out earlier, said, "You can wade out in this. The water isn't fast moving. If you go now, I'll pick you up at the end of the road."

As I hung up the phone from talking to him, I felt like I should wade out immediately, not to wait. I grabbed my oldest boy who was about 19 at the time. We walked to the water's edge and my son put my suitcase on top of his head. I carried my computer in a backpack on my back. I had a set of chest waders on. My son just had jeans and a white t-shirt.

My brother-in-law told me it wouldn't go to my waist, but when we stepped in and walked a few feet, it was immediately to my waist. I'm 5'10" and my son is 6'2". We went a little further and it was up to our armpits.

The whole while I was holding my computer backpack on my head praying in my mind, "Please don't let me drop the laptop, please don't let me drop the laptop, please don't let me drop the laptop."

I walked behind my son, staying alert for potholes in the dirt/gravel road. One dip or stumble and I could drop my computer equipment. The water seeped into the waders, and I felt like I was moon walking down the half-mile drive.

Had I not known that I needed to take that trip to Utah, I would not have gotten in the water. But I knew it was something I needed to do. Fortunately, my son and I, my suitcase and my laptop made it to the other side. I made it safely to Utah. That is when I met Martina Muir and got to know Judy Rankin. It proved to be pivotal in my life.

This little story illustrates the HALO over Gratitude formula. It shows the importance of getting a confirmation about what you need to be doing and that you're on the right path. Once you have that, you can swiftly act with confidence when the Spirit tells you to do so. There was only a small window in which I could have walked out because the waters continued to rise and didn't go down for over a week. If I had not acted when I did, it would have been too dangerous.

Conclusion

I hope as you conclude this book that you are coming away with greater confidence in trusting your instincts, your intuition, your inspiration.

I hope you know how much you are loved by God. He wants you to have answers to your questions. He wants to help you fulfill your life's work. He would love nothing more than to help you succeed in blessing the lives of those around you by helping you tap into your gifts and allow His Spirit to flow through you.

I hope you know that God wants to bless you in your business, and that He loves it when you proactively seek to magnify Him in your chosen life's work.

I hope you have come away with some strategies and tools for how to allow the Spirit to guide you in your business and in your life's work.

I hope some of the practical experience and advice I've shared about business can help you avoid some of the typical pitfalls many of us encounter, like:

- undervaluing ourselves
- not trusting our guts when they tell us to turn down a client or a project
- getting involved with charismatic people who make big promises but don't deliver
- not being consistent enough to see success
- not being willing to adapt, tweak, and track our results until we achieve our desired outcome
- caring too much about our competition or comparing ourselves to others
- not utilizing the power of delegation and trying to do it all ourselves

I hope you come away knowing how to:

- tap into inspiration in a powerful way
- get answers to your pressing problems
- discover your pivot point and stick with it so you have focus and direction
- create multiple income streams
- leverage the power of relationships and Quantum Collaboration to magnify your influence and success
- be true to yourself and who you are
- act when inspiration comes
- work with your creative cycle and understand where you are at any given point within it.

If I could give you one last parting piece of advice, it would be to ask to see your business through God's eyes. Anytime I feel like I can't see my way forward or answers aren't coming, I ask God to help me see the situation or my business through His eyes. What are the opportunities I'm not seeing? How should I reframe a situation to see it from a new angle or perspective? Please remove the blinders or clouds from my vision. This is one of the most powerful prayers. Try it and expect answers! In the right time and way, you will begin to see things with new clarity and insight.

Get Your Free Consult

If you would like to discuss your Spirit-led business with me, please hop on my calendar for a free 20-minute strategy session. You can get that by going to MarnieKuhns.com/spirit20

About the Author

Marnie Pehrson Kuhns is a Certified SimplyHealed Practitioner™ who uses music and creativity to mentor you past barriers, fears and doubts to discover, create and deliver your soul's song (the mission, message or purpose you are on this earth to live).

Marnie is also a bestselling author who leads Trust Your Heart Groups to help you tap into your divine knowing, your soul's song, and live a life you'll love.

Marnie is a mother of 6 and grandmother who started her own business back in May of 1990. She's published 27 titles including historical fiction romance, inspirational Christian and business books. Her book, *Confidence Rising! Trust Your Heart. Be Yourself. Bless Lives* shares her miraculous story of overcoming devastating losses to restoration and recovery. www.TrustYourHeartSeries.com

Marnie believes you are here to express something that is uniquely you in the world — whether it's in your daily interactions with family and friends, in a book, through music or art, or a business. You matter!

The world needs you and your gifts! Marnie's mission is to help you tap into and share your uniqueness in a way that is right for you.

Marnie and her husband, Dave, live in Northwest Georgia where they conduct Passion Retreats that help you listen to your heart, tap into your soul's song and express your creativity. www.PassionRetreats.com

To set up a free 20-minute strategy session with Marnie, click here. Marnie may also be reached by email at marnie@marniekuhns.com.

Non-Fiction

- *Restoring Liberty: Personal Freedom and Responsibility in America*
- *Confidence Rising! Trust Your Heart. Be Yourself. Bless Lives*
- *Trust Your Heart: Transforming Your Ideas Into Income*
- *Trust Your Heart: Building Relationships That Build Your Business*
- *Light the World: How Your Brilliance Can Shift the Planet*
- *You're Here for a Reason: Discover and Live Your Purpose*
- *You Can't Fly If You're Still Clutching the Dirt*
- *10 Steps to Fulfilling Your Divine Destiny*

- *Lord, Are You Sure?*
- *Packets of Sunlight for Parents*
- *Packets of Sunlight for American Patriots*

Find these books and more on Amazon at www.MarnieKuhns.com/marniesbooks

Historical

- *The Patriot Wore Petticoats* (Revolutionary War)
- *An Uncertain Justice* (1920s true story about the last legal hanging in Georgia)
- *Angel and the Enemy* (Civil War historical fiction romance)
- *Hannah's Heart* (historical romance)
- *Rebecca's Reveries* (Post Civil War historical romance)
- *Beyond the Waterfall* (Trail of Tears historical romance)

Find these books and more on Amazon at www.MarnieKuhns.com/marniesbooks/

Southern Romance

- *Savannah Nights*
- *Binding Ties*
- *In Love We Trust / Second Sight*

Find these books and more on Amazon at MarnieKuhns.com/marniesbooks

Find more books and get information on publishing your own books at SpiritTreePublishing.com

People Mentioned In This Book

- **David Kuhns** – my husband who does editing, copywriting, marketing, training development, etc. www.CyranoWriter.com
- **Joyce Pierce** – attended the Light the World Retreat and proofread this book - www.facebook.com/letmeproof/
- **Leslie Householder** – taught me the laws of thought - www.ThoughtsAlive.com
- **Carolyn Cooper** – creator of the SimplyHealed Method™ www.SimplyHealed.com
- **Phillip Davis** – naming and branding expert who taught me about pivot points and more - www.TungstenBranding.com
- **Luanna Rodham-** my right-arm at IdeaMarketers.com who helped me with day-to-day aspects of the site. Without delegating to her and brainstorming with her it wouldn't have grown into the success it became EasyBreezyMarketing.com
- **Judy Rankin** – taught me how to use guided meditation and co-created the Light the World Retreat - www.TrustingSpiritNow.com

- **Sheldon Pickering** – pianist who performed and taught at the Light the World Retreat - www.SheldonPickering.com
- **Jamie Bartschi** – violinist who performed and taught at the Light the World Retreat - JamieMusician.com
- **Martina Muir** – my talented energy practitioner friend who I got to know at Leslie Householder's writer retreat and who helped fill our Light the World Retreat - IAmLivingLight.com

Made in the USA
Coppell, TX
08 July 2020

30455919R00115